Praise for

— MORE THAN THE —
Tattooed
MORMON

"Amazing lady! Amazing conversion! This is a story about not just what's outside but what's inside. It's a story not just about judging but about not being offended. Al shares her story with frankness and passion. She fills each chapter with memorable insights and true wisdom. But this book isn't really about Al. It is about God and you! It is about the transformation that is possible for all of us through the Atonement of Jesus Christ."

—Brad Wilcox, PhD, professor at Brigham Young University, author of *The Continuous Atonement* and *The Continuous Conversion*

"Al's pure goodness and enthusiasm for the gospel fill her new book, *More Than the Tattooed Mormon*. Once I started reading, I couldn't put it down! I'm thrilled she wrote her compelling, uplifting story—telling it in her own honest, frank, and real way. Her change of heart changed mine. It caused me to think deeply and reflect on my own journey. Al Fox Carraway is a cheerleader for faith in the Savior and hope in the Atonement. She is on fire with the spirit of missionary work. And because of her courage and dedication, she is touching hundreds of lives along the way."

—Michelle King, television producer and host, former host of Mormon Times TV

"If you think you already know all there is to know about the Al Carraway story, think again. Al delivers her journey in the gospel with a zest rarely seen in Mormon memoirs. Even on the page her energy is so contagious that you find yourself moving from the sidelines, cheering her on as she recounts her trials and triumphs, to being motivated to put some pep in your step in your own walk with God. Al Carraway is truly *More Than the Tattooed Mormon*, this sista is a cheerleader for Jesus, and instead of waving pom-poms, she's moving with the power of the Spirit."

—Zandra Vranes and Tamu Smith, authors of SISTASinZION.com and *Diary of Two Mad Black Mormons*

"Al Fox Carraway is a wonderfully fresh combination of energy, humor, and testimony. At first, you might think this book is all about Al. But the more you read, the more you will find personal motivation to keep going, to keep trying, and to stay close to the Lord through all of life's challenges."

—John Bytheway, author of *How Do I Know If I Know?*

"If you put this book back on the bookstore shelf, you are making a huge mistake. In these pages, Al takes you on one of the most faith-building journeys you'll ever experience. Al is real. Al is authentic. You'll come away from this book adoring Al (especially her stubborn New Yorker attitude), but more important, Al's story will bring you closer to Christ."

—Hank Smith, PhD, bestselling LDS author
and speaker, BYU religion instructor

"Al's story is powerful because it allows you to personally walk through the process of conversion with her from start to finish. Whether you are just starting on your pathway to following Christ or continuing a life-long journey, this book will deepen your desire to believe. Filled with scriptures, prophetic counsel, and a beautiful testimony of grace, Al's story will leave in imprint on your heart that won't soon be forgotten."

—Emily Belle Freeman, author of *Even This*

"I devoured it. Al is so loveable. Her openness and sincerity make you feel like she's telling you her story from across the room. I'm inspired by her determination to follow her heart, even when it was driving her somewhere that her family and friends—and even she herself—didn't think she should or could go. She's a breath of fresh air these days when it seems everyone wants to go their own direction—but Al chooses to boldly follow the Lord."

—Jessica Gee, travel journalist of *The Bucket List Family*

MORE THAN THE

Tattooed MORMON

SECOND EDITION

AL CARRAWAY

CFI

AN IMPRINT OF CEDAR FORT, INC.
SPRINGVILLE, UTAH

Cover photo courtesy of Rebecca Price of bekapricephotography.com.

ISBN 13: 978-1-4621-2227-1 (paperback)
ISBN 13: 978-1-4621-2176-2 (hardback)

Published by CFI, an imprint of Cedar Fort, Inc.
2373 W. 700 S., Springville, UT 84663
Distributed by Cedar Fort, Inc., www.cedarfort.com

The Library of Congress has cataloged the previous edition as follows:

Carraway, Al, 1988- author.
More than the tattooed Mormon / Al Carraway.
pages cm
Includes bibliographical references.
ISBN 978-1-4621-1720-8 (hardback : alk. paper)
1. Carraway, Al, 1988- 2. Mormon women--Biography. I. Title.

BX8695.C275A3 2015
289.3092--dc23
[B]

2015020177

Cover design and layout by Shawnda T. Craig

Edited by Jessica B. Ellingson, Kathryn Watkins, and Kaitlin Barwick

Printed in the United States of America

10 9 8 7 6 5 4 3 2 1

Printed on acid-free paper

Dedicated to
the reader

Also by Al Carraway

Cheers to Eternity:
Lessons We've Learned on
Dating and Marriage

I Know journal

Set Goals. Say Prayers. Work Hard. journal

With God, Life Is Oh So Good journal

More than the Tattooed Mormon
is now also available as an audio CD,
read by the author.

Table of Contents

Faith in Christ can help you resolv
personal and family challenges.

Please accept this
free DVD,
Finding Faith in Chris
Call
1-800-443-9911

1/2 a steak
Elder Cox & Elder Obi
414-2516

THE CHURCH OF
JESUS CHRIST
OF LATTER-DAY SAINTS

www.mormon.org

I AM ONE OF THOSE RESCUED

Part 1

- My Story -

Chapter 1 . . .

HAPPY LIFE

> If I were given a chance to change any
> aspect of my life growing up,
> I WOULDN'T TAKE IT.

LIFE BEFORE THE CHURCH seemed to be great, actually—filled with incredible memories and countless traditions. I'm the baby of three girls. I have a sister just a year older than me, Cierra, who has been my best friend and biggest cheerleader. At every age of my life, I was pretty spontaneous and the one who gave my parents the most gray hair. I always had a new idea of something to do and try—some logical, most not—and she was the one who always, with excitement, had my back no matter what. I was close with my oldest sister, Rachel, who is only four years older than me, but it was just enough of a gap for an awkward age separation growing up. I definitely looked up to her though. I looked at her life and tried to mimic it. She was so cool to me—much cooler than Britney Spears, which at that time was a hefty statement. My sister was my role model for so long, right up to about junior high, when my stubbornness kicked into full gear and I decided I wanted to be my own role model.

My parents separated when I was young, but that never bothered me, and it never affected how they acted toward my two sisters and me. Sometimes I liked to think it was better that way because there was hardly any fighting in our family, unless it was when my sisters caught me stealing their clothes.

My mom is in the dental field, and she did everything you could think of for us girls—being the head of the PTA, our cheerleading coach, and even our Girl Scout leader. She drove us to every hobby and sport we wanted to indulge in, including gymnastics, horseback riding, and faraway soccer games. Whatever we did, she was involved. Up until the day each of us moved out, she woke us up with hot chocolate and breakfast. No matter how small the holiday or occasion, my mom celebrates it *big*. I'm talking "the *whole* house in complete party decoration" big. She was who we lived with and the wheel that kept us all moving forward. At one point she worked three jobs at once because she wanted to give us everything she could. Whenever I felt like being lazy with life, she was there to not just motivate me but also help me every step of the way to discover that there was something more to me and I really could do and be great in anything I chose.

East Coast culture and my mom's side of the family are where I gained most of my personality. Our family gatherings with my aunt and cousins were frequent and always very loud. We were close-knit, and no matter what we were doing together it was *always* a party. The smallest and simplest of things were exciting. My mom and her side of the family all speak their minds and are always honest. Usually that was a good thing, but sometimes not, and it was my dad who taught me how to do so in the best way.

Although we didn't live with my dad, we saw him all the time, whenever we wanted. If you asked him the best thing about his life, his answer would be the times he spent with us. He was always looking for things to do with us and went to absolutely everything we ever did. Even for the small, lame successes that probably didn't have reason to be celebrated, he was there and he was really proud. It wasn't just that my sisters and I were all daddy's girls; it was much more than that. He is someone everyone wants to be around. As I got older, my friends would leave me to go hang out with my dad. My dad is an artist—a painter. He taught us manners, about humor and art, to embrace culture and differences, and to explore creatively. He taught me a love for the outdoors, a love of learning, a love of reading, and a respect for *all* people. He was constantly bringing us to new places and letting us meet new people. I never wanted to get married, mainly because it just wasn't a goal for most people in our culture. But if I ever did, I knew I wanted to marry a clone of my dad.

If I were given a chance to change any aspect of my life growing up, I wouldn't take it. Even with the kinks of family life and life in general that everyone has—ours were usually financial—I'm confident saying that it may not have been anywhere close to perfect, but it was perfect *for me*. I am who I am today because of what they taught me and because of who they were and are. Because of the life they created for me, I find great joy in the simplicities of life, and that has been one of my favorite takeaways from them.

My life without the gospel is most definitely notable; it shaped me. But that's not how I want this story to start. I want to start when everything I thought I knew about life was questioned and challenged. I want to start with my realization that a lot of what I concluded about life was wrong.

Life was different growing up in New York, but it was the only life I knew—and I loved it. I grew up in upstate New York in a big city called Rochester. It was definitely *not* New York City. It was much more green than you are probably thinking but had a lot of the same quirks people associate with NYC. No matter where you went, food was going to be incredible.

You would buy chicken wings for every occasion, with a lot of pizza on the side. Our most notable entrée was the garbage plate—your choice of hamburger meat or hot dog meat (or both), piled with steak fries, macaroni salad, sometimes beans, meat sauce, and hot sauce on top. No matter the season, there were several festivals going on or exhibits to visit every week. There was a little bit of everything all around, and it was perfect. Everyone celebrated differences and spoke his or her mind but was still full of acceptance.

If you were to ask anyone that lived there if happiness was real or lasting, I'm not sure they would say yes, but that seemed to be normal in our culture—just accepting having glimpses of it pass by. But I'm pretty sure if you asked me, I would tell you I was the closest anyone was ever going to get to having real happiness.

My culture and family taught me to work hard and just make things happen. At age twenty, I honestly thought I had my whole life figured out. I had big goals, the drive to accomplish all of them, and the stubbornness to do it all alone. I didn't need help from anyone or anything, and definitely not from religion. I was right where I wanted to be. Every day I learned more of my passion with art that my dad had sparked in me and my sisters, and I graduated college with my degree in graphic design. I worked full time. I was launching my own business doing event photography. And I had my very own studio apartment—granted it was a very small apartment (no bigger than most public bathrooms), but it was mine and I loved every ten-by-fifteen feet of it.

It was no longer than a week or two after moving out of my ex-boyfriend's house and into that bathroom-sized apartment—having thoughts of "I have life in the palm of my hands right now"—that life was forever going to change for me.

Chapter 2 . . .

ASK GOD, NOT GOOGLE

> I FOUND MYSELF CARING.
> I found myself needing to know if the Church was true, because if it wasn't, why keep going, right?

I WAS OUTSIDE HELPING someone move when I saw these two guys riding bikes come around the corner, and they were dressed *really nice*. My first thought was, *Who wears helmets still?*

They came up to us and said, "Do you want to know more about Christ?" I didn't, and I may have let out an audible laugh as my answer. The person I was helping move knew who they were: missionaries. He was so mean to them! I just felt so bad (I think it was because I thought they looked so precious with their goofy bike helmets and button-up shirts), but not bad enough to actually listen to them. I told them that if they brought me a steak to eat, I'd listen. Surely that would get rid of them, right? I gave them my address, thinking it was the most clever answer anyone could have come up with to nicely decline, because who would actually do that?

It was that *same* day, as I was sitting outside on my porch, that I saw the boys with the goofy helmets come down my street. I was completely surprised by what I saw. They not only had a steak for me but also a stack of pamphlets and a Book of Mormon. Do you believe it? I felt obligated to let them say whatever it was they wanted to say before I got rid of them one last and final time. I mean, they did bring me a steak.

I grew up Catholic, like most everyone else where I'm from. My grandma was devout, and my mom grew up going to an all-girls Catholic school and had to learn Latin. My dad was not religious at all but wanted us girls to learn some sort of morals from somewhere. And really what that meant was that we went to church (or Mass, as we called it) *maybe* for Christmas and Easter. I don't remember too much of what was actually said at church, but I do remember that I had to shake hands with strangers and say, "Peace be with you." I was always anxious to stand up toward the end and stand in line to eat this tasteless wafer, because it was a sign that we were close to going out to breakfast afterward.

I knew of Christ and some major highlights of His life, but I didn't know anyone was supposed to do anything because of it. They were nothing more than stories of someone's life, no different than the story of my neighbor's life, both of which I didn't care to learn more about.

I thought religion was something people turned to only when things were going wrong in their lives. It was just something that people relied on for some sort of mental comfort because life was hard and there were endless problems. But not me. There was nothing I thought I couldn't handle on my own. So I smiled and nodded and pretended to listen to the boys with goofy helmets for a lot longer than I probably should have until they left.

I was in the clear! So I thought. But the strangest thing happened. As soon as they left, I wanted them to come back. It was just *something* about them. I felt this pull, and almost without even realizing it, I was calling them moments after they left (they wrote their number on absolutely everything), because I wanted them to come back. They didn't make it that far either; I could still see them on my street when I called them back and asked when I could see them again.

"When you read," they said.

"What if I don't want to do that? What else ya got?"

I started to read every day out of the Book of Mormon just so I could see them every day, and I did. I sat on my porch every morning with my cup of coffee, and I fake listened to them. I didn't want to listen; I just wanted them around. I would try so hard to talk about anything *except* what they wanted to talk about, and I thought I was doing really well at that. Looking back on this, it's obvious it was the Spirit they had with them that I just wanted to feel and be around. It was the Spirit we receive as a gift when we are confirmed members of the Church—the same Spirit we sometimes take for granted because of the very real promise to us that He can be with us always. Well, I had never recognized or felt the Spirit before, and the difference is real.

One day they came over and asked to watch a video, and I thought, *YES! They get it; I don't care what they have to say. Finally a break from all this religious stuff. Put that movie in, boys. This is great!*

Go figure, it was a Church movie. I should have seen that coming. I didn't. It was called *The Restoration*, and it was about the First Vision. The whole time I watched it, I was just in awe, but not a good awe. No way did these things in the movie happen. No way did this place even exist. All I wanted to do was prove the elders wrong, that's it. So I said in mock, in challenge, "Hey, boys, I want to go there," thinking I couldn't. And do you know what they said to me?

"Oh, you can. You're, like, forty minutes away."

I learned a great lesson that day: Al, keep your mouth shut.

We went to Palmyra, New York, and I had no idea this place existed—and it was in my backyard, practically. There was nothing out there, just farmland, and there were license plates from all different states in the parking lot. I was so confused why anyone would want to travel so far to come to the middle of nowhere and look at farmland.

If you haven't met me, one of the things you should know about me is that I love to talk. I love to talk about everything (except, at the time, the Church), and I love to talk to everyone, especially complete strangers. But this day I just couldn't speak. I was tongue-tied, and that never happens. I was quiet, so quiet that it actually freaked me out. Half the time I was actually listening to what these girls were saying and wondering why they were wearing skirts, because I didn't even own one or ever have any need to own one except maybe for a funeral, and the other half of the time I was internally freaking out and wondering why I was acting so weird.

We made it to the Sacred Grove, and my elders turned to me and said, "We should pray. We should pray because of what happened here and because of the Spirit that there is."

I had never felt more awkward in my entire life than I did in that exact moment. I turned to my elders, and I laughed so hard. I laughed, and I could not stop laughing for the life of me.

I had never said a prayer before in my life. In the Catholic Church, the priest does all the talking, and then there are two prayers that I know of that we repeated all the time for everything. They were repeated so much it was hard to know it was even a prayer at all. I am not kidding, it was minutes of me laughing because of how uncomfortable I was at just the thought of praying. And with all my laughing, it became awkward for everyone, I'm sure.

The elders very generously asked, "Al, what are you doing? We'll say the prayer, and you just repeat after us. That's it, just repeat after us."

I closed my eyes and then opened one to look at them to see how I should stand and what to do with my arms. While they were praying, and as I repeated after them, I just kept thinking how embarrassed I was that we were standing there with our eyes closed, just talking out loud to what I thought was no one.

And that was the first time I ever spoke to my Father in Heaven. In the Sacred Grove. And can you imagine how I felt?

I went home and sat in the middle of my bathroom-sized apartment. (Not like I had any other option anyway. I literally could not fit a chair in there—that's how small it was.) And I felt . . . terrible. I felt absolutely terrible. I'm not much of a crier—I just don't cry that often—but I was hysterical. I couldn't stop crying for the life of me.

I am not exaggerating when I say this lasted for hours; I was just consumed with all this anxiety, and fear, and who knows what else. I didn't know what to do. I didn't know what was happening; I had never felt anything like that before in my life, and I couldn't make it stop. I think it was the first time I felt and recognized this darkness.

I called my elders because I honestly thought they were the smartest boys in the world. They came up with an answer to everything. I yelled at them, saying, "I don't know what to do! I don't know why I feel this way!" And do you know what they told me to do?

Pray.

"I'm not doing that. Do you remember what just happened in that forest? I'm not doing that again."

"Yes, you are, and don't call us back until you do."

And then they hung up on me.

I became desperate. On top of my fridge were those pamphlets I swore I would never read. And in the back of every single pamphlet it teaches you, in bullet points, how to say a prayer. I hadn't the slightest idea how to say one.

I opened it up, put it on my bed, knelt down, interlocked my fingers, and kept one eye open to peek at the pamphlet because I didn't want to do it wrong. And I had what I *know* to be the worst prayer Heavenly Father has ever heard. Ever. I have no idea what I said, and I know for a fact I didn't get any answers to my questions. But what I do know is that when I stopped praying, I stopped crying. It was a very small feeling, but I felt like things were going to be okay.

I woke up the next morning and found out (against my will) that not only is Heavenly Father real, but He also answers prayers. My elders made me ask if the Church was true (because I was repeating after them). And it wasn't until then, saying it in prayer, that I found myself caring. I found myself needing to know if the Church was true, because if it wasn't, why keep going, right?

You have to know, I did not want the Church to be true at all; not even a sliver of it did I want to be true. Because if it were, that meant I would have to change. I'd have to change absolutely everything—not just what I did; even the way I thought had to be different. I didn't want to change. I loved who I was. I loved who I was and what I was doing. If I changed, I wouldn't be me anymore. That's what I thought.

Chapter 3 . . .
CHANGE & BAPTISM

We are BLESSED
by our EFFORTS of trying,
not perfection.

I STARTED TO CHANGE unconsciously because of the simple things of the gospel. I was praying what I thought were the worst prayers Heavenly Father had ever heard. And I was reading who-knows-what out of the Book of Mormon; it made no sense to me at first. But it's promised to us that if we do those things, if we just *try*, we become better.

Other people started to notice this change before I ever did. Before the thought of baptism even entered into my mind at all, I kept hearing the same thing. My good friend Gilly told me, "Al, you look good."

I was so confused. I answered, "Uhh . . . thanks? I'm wearing a new shirt?"

"That's not it," he said. "Whatever you are doing, do not stop."

I thought, *Eh? The only thing I am doing is praying the worst prayers Heavenly Father has ever heard and, you know, reading who-knows-what out of that blue book the boys with the goofy helmets gave me.*

So many people started telling me that that I finally decided to try. A *real* try. I still had the intent that I was just going to prove the elders wrong. But the only way to do that was to actually live what they taught me and show them that nothing would happen. I made a promise to myself that I was going to learn as much as I could, do my best to do what I could with exactness, and, most important, do it long enough to allow room for contrast and change. I started to highlight and write down notes and questions from reading. I started to not only listen during my lessons with the elders but also actually ask questions. I continued to pray with one eye open with my pamphlet in front of me a few times a day. And the most terrifying thing of all, I found myself defending the Church. It was in the moment I caught myself saying to others, "Well, actually they don't believe that. They believe this," that I started thinking, *Uh-oh, what's happening to me?*

After several weeks of avoiding the invitation of going to church, coming up with every excuse I could think of each week, I finally decided to go, you know, to prove the elders wrong. And it was extremely stressful. I never had a reason to wear a dress or skirt, and I didn't even own either of them, with the exception of a black, strapless sundress you wear over a bathing suit. I wore that.

In a perfect world, I would have sat all the way in the back to observe and sneak out when it was ending. But as I would learn very quickly with this new relationship I was starting with God, things would hardly go how I had in mind. My elders were ASL elders (American Sign Language) and had to sit in the front row and take turns interpreting the meeting for the deaf. Not only did I not get to sneak in, but they were also late, and we had to parade from the back all the way up to the front in front of everyone. It was awful. I felt like people could just smell that I didn't belong there somehow. I didn't listen to a single thing that was said during the entire meeting, and I refused to sing one note of any hymn. I was too concerned with how uncomfortable I felt being at church; it was just so out of character for me.

My elders asked with great excitement, "So what'd you think?"

"I hated it. No way am I going back again next week, so don't bother asking."

And I meant it.

Yet there I was exactly a week later, standing in front of my closet, realizing I still didn't have a dress to wear to church. Before I knew what I was doing, I already had the same black, strapless beach dress on and was driving back to church.

That's how this all started. My transformation came just from the act of doing and trying. With my flawed and mostly awkward efforts to live the way the gospel taught me, I found myself overcoming. I found myself conquering. I was overcoming and conquering things I *never* thought I would overcome and conquer. Things I thought I would be stuck with and struggle with for the rest of my life. Habits I had tried *so* many times previous to quit and couldn't do it. Things that just made me "who I was." I'll talk about this more specifically in a later chapter.

If you asked the missionaries, they'd tell you I was the last person they thought would do this. But I changed. That three-word sentence seems simple and small, but don't be mistaken: it wasn't easy. But it was *easier*, because this time around I had help. I had prayer. This time I had real reason and purpose. This was the first time I had noticed God in my life. This was the first time I had noticed hard things in life were easier because of my efforts, no matter how "off" I thought they were. This was the first time I realized that we are blessed by our efforts, not perfection. This was the beginning of me knowing that the gospel is not there to prevent hard times from happening but to make those hard times doable and easier.

I changed—not because someone told me I had to; that wouldn't have worked with me. Stubborn New Yorker, remember? Whether or not I recognized what it was at the time, I changed because that is what happens when you *feel* the Spirit. That is what happens when Christ becomes a reality to you. You change because then you *want* to and because then you can.

I was changing slowly and daily since the day I met the elders. I changed, and to my surprise, I never changed into someone else. I truly felt like I'd found my real *me*—who I was meant to be all along.

I would get home late enough from work some nights that the nightlife I lived right in the middle of was starting to settle down and become quiet. I'd walk my dog around a few blocks before it was time to go to bed. The strangely quiet city seemed to trigger these heavy questions I had never thought of until I met the boys with goofy helmets, and they began to trigger thoughts and ideas that never came to mind until I started praying. Many nights were spent and many blocks were walked looking up at the sky with this physical pull toward the thought of something more to life. Something more to me.

Days were spent reading and studying, and nights were spent continually trying to wrap my head around everything. Gospel. God. Life. Life in the hereafter. Was there really a cure to my biggest fear: death? A fear that was so real and vivid and scary that I'd have to look away when passing cemeteries because of the severe uneasiness it brought to my mind.

I woke up at 4:00 a.m. one morning, and I could not go back to bed. I just couldn't sleep for the life of me, so what did I do? I called my elders. They were the smartest boys in the world, remember? Because they came up with an answer for everything, surely they'd be able to tell me why I couldn't sleep, right?

I didn't know what I was going to say to them because I didn't think they'd actually answer. What elder answers the phone at four o'clock in the morning? For that matter, what person anywhere would answer that early? I called thinking they wouldn't pick up. They did.

My first reaction, the first thing I thought of to do was to just start yelling at them, "I WANT TO GET BAPTIZED!"

Wait . . . What?

I had no idea that's what I was going to say. Surely, I had no idea that's even what I wanted to do! When I said it—well, when I *yelled* it—I felt it. I *knew* that was what I needed to do. I got so embarrassed I just hung up the phone on them.

Could you image that phone call? Four in the morning, just being yelled at, the word *baptism* in there somewhere, and then click. Like, wait, what? I am not kidding, this came out of nowhere; my elders called me right back, and they were more confused than excited.

"Wait, what? Why? What happened?" They were so confused and caught off guard that you couldn't even tell in their voices that I had just woken them up. If you ever went on a mission and had those investigators you thought were going nowhere—that was me.

So I decided to get baptized, and that was wild. Even though I knew this decision was right, even though I could physically feel that the Church was true, I was embarrassed. I was ashamed to be a part of anything dealing with the gospel—so embarrassed and ashamed that I didn't invite a single person to my baptism.

Okay, I invited one person. His name was Scott. At the time I didn't really know who Scott was, so it was really awkward. He was dating my oldest sister at the time, but I didn't know anything other than that.

"Hey, kinda getting baptized . . ."

"Can I come?"

"I think that's why I called you? Yeah, you can come."

Getting baptized was also wild because there was still so much I didn't know. Out of everything there is to know about this church, the *only* thing that I knew was that the Book of Mormon was true. And I didn't even read it all the way through. I'm not even sure I got through more than a handful of chapters before I could just *feel* that how I felt within those few chapters made not only the whole book true but also the whole church. It wasn't naïve of me. It might not have made logical sense, but the Spirit is not always logical; it's spiritual—my number one rule when following a prompting.

But why couldn't I get tattoos? And why couldn't gays get married? And who was this Holland guy, and why did everyone talk about him so much? I had so many questions that were important to me that I didn't understand because of my culture growing up. But because of the help I noticed I was getting from God with my small and awkward efforts, I was eager to keep going and to see what else He could do for me when I was actually a part of His Church, trying to do everything He wanted me to do. Those questions I had weren't enough to hold me back. I was still going to get baptized, knowing that I would find out more along the way, and whatever those answers were they would be right, regardless of my narrow and prideful thoughts.

Those answers did come, but not in the way I thought they would. I found that the more I read, the more I learned; the more I acted and served and grew in the gospel, the more the questions I had disappeared on their own, and my vision, thoughts, outlook, and desires changed. I literally woke up one day and everything just clicked. I woke up one day and anything I ever disagreed with, or desires I had that were not in line with the gospel, disappeared on their own. He gave me understanding, comfort, and knowledge. It was like the clouds blocking some of the sun had disappeared and cleared up.

I have not gotten a tattoo since I was baptized, nor do I plan to or ever want to. The desire is not there like I thought it would be. My interest in that is completely and absolutely gone. That's how it will be with anything not in line with the gospel. That's a promise to us: the more we try and the more we turn to Him and the more we learn, we will be changed and become more like Him.

After the phone call that surprised not only the missionaries but also myself, my elders came over bright and early that same day and were anxious to pick a date for my baptism. That's when reality set in, and butterflies came that never seemed to leave until after the ordinance.

My elders suggested I pick a baptism date on a Saturday so I could get confirmed the next day in church. Twenty-two is my favorite number. It's a number that I just happen to notice all the time, and everything seems to happen around that date. So I joked, saying that whenever the twenty-second fell on a Saturday of whichever month or year, then I would follow through with it. I should have been surprised that it was only two weeks away, but with how things seemed to be panning out, I wasn't.

I decided this would be the occasion to finally buy a proper dress or skirt. Naturally, I went to Target because, I mean, it's Target. I wandered around the women's clothing section like a lost puppy. I didn't realize how hard it was to find something modest that someone under the age of sixty would wear. I actually turned to an employee for help because I was struggling so much. He asked what it was for, and I was still so embarrassed to say I was getting baptized that I didn't answer him. What I wore to my baptism was actually picked out by this seventeen-year-old guy I hunted down from the electronics department in desperation.

I hadn't invited anyone to my baptism except Scott, but the room was *packed* with people. And that meant the world to me. Them just being there—that's it, just being there—was a testimony to me that what I was doing was right.

I was so anxious, and my mind was racing because I just barely caught glimpse of myself in a transition of my life. Usually change happens either so fast or so gradually that it's hard to catch it in the moment and take a breath to embrace it. I was afraid that because I caught a glimpse of that moment I would change my mind, so I paced around the church building by myself. I saw Scott pull in and was completely surprised to see my oldest sister, Rachel, who was pagan at the time, step out of the car. Embarrassment came in full physical force. Then the mission president came, and my elders came outside and said it was past the hour and everyone was waiting on me.

I sat on the first row next to my elders, Elder Despain dressed in white with me. He wouldn't look at me, but he was smiling and crying. I looked up to see someone from my singles branch saying a few remarks on baptism, and she was crying too. I didn't want to cry, so I just looked down at my and my elder's bare feet. That's when it hit me.

I was completely consumed and thought, *This is happiness. This* is real and *physical* and lasting happiness. Regardless of not listening to the message the elders were sharing with me at first, I *knew* that they had something I didn't. Regardless of this "happiness" I *thought* I had before, I didn't. I had never felt anything like how I felt in that exact moment. I'd never even felt a sliver of what I was feeling then. I didn't realize how fake and fleeting what I had before was until I felt this. I felt alive! Though, is it any wonder I felt that way? "He is the light and the life of the world; yea, a light that is endless, that can never be darkened; yea, and also a life which is endless, that there can be no more death" (Mosiah 16:9). Christ is the Light and *Life* of this world, here, where we are right now. In order to truly live we must turn to Him. *"We are made alive in Christ"* (2 Nephi 25:25).

Do you remember getting confirmed—getting the gift of the Holy Ghost? I do. And it's not because it happened later in my life but because that was my absolute favorite part; I loved it! When I got that gift, when those hands touched my head, I *physically* felt myself get that gift. The difference is real. The contrast is huge! In that exact second, I was not embarrassed anymore, I was not ashamed anymore in any degree, and I wanted to yell to all of New York that happiness is real! It exists! They *can* have it; I have these boys with goofy helmets, and we'll talk to ya! God is real, and He in reality speaks to us. How could anything in life go wrong, right?

Chapter 4 . . .

SO RIGHT, BUT SO HARD

> Hard times will consistently be there,
> BUT SO WILL CHRIST.

IN THE VISION LEHI had, once he made it to the tree of life, the first thing he wanted to do was share it with his family (1 Nephi 8:15). That's what a realization of the gospel does to people.

Naturally when you have something you love, when you have something that makes you feel good, you want to share it, right? You want to share it with the people you care most about in life—your friends, your family. So I turned to my friends. I feel like I had a lot of friends, and I did; I had a lot of friends. Friends that I loved, friends that I grew up with my whole life, friends that I trusted and would tell everything to. But not one friend stayed.

Not one.

They *all* left. They wanted nothing to do with me and what I was a part of.

It hurt. It hurt to see all of them leave and how easily and quickly they did. Though thinking back on it now, as upset and offended and hurt as I was, I'm not sure what I'd have had in common with them anymore even if one of them did stay. Most problems you deal with in life are not even variables to those who are members of the Church. I wouldn't want to sit through any more conversations of who drank too much the night previous and whom they accidentally slept with because of it. But that didn't ease those incredibly strong and almost daily feelings of loneliness—a completely new and unfamiliar feeling for me.

I'd go to work: parking enforcement at the hospital. I was the one who sat in those small booths outside a parking garage, making you pay. Regardless of being the most hated at the hospital (who wants to hear they have to pay ten dollars for parking for only an hour after hearing someone in their family just passed away?), I loved my job. I loved seeing hundreds of people a day and challenged myself to try and make the person in each car that went through my booth smile. I had a fake cop uniform I wore—men's white button-up shirt; tie, which I could tie all on my own; and men's dress pants, which were the most unflattering pair of pants a girl could ever want to put on. They were huge. Even though I wasn't allowed to read on the job, I hid the Book of Mormon completely in the front of my pants, and you couldn't tell it was there—that's how big those pants were.

I worked with the funniest people you could imagine. I loved them. But after I got baptized, I would leave my booth for the night and a few times my coworkers and my boss would get together and lock me in their office. While I was locked in, they would yell at me, "You are *not* a good person! What you are doing? What you are a part of *is* wrong!" Then they'd make me watch all of these terrible videos about the Church.

How hard that was. I didn't know how to defend the Church or myself. I was *just barely* baptized, and the only thing I knew was that those few chapters from the Book of Mormon made the whole Church true. I felt like I was being punished for doing what I thought was the right thing, and I felt like I couldn't escape from any of it. It was coming from all directions and from everyone around me.

So then I turned to my family.

My dad was my best friend. We were the closest you could ever imagine. He lived above a popular restaurant in this awesome apartment with a balcony that looked out over the best street in downtown Rochester. It's where all the galleries and cafes were and where the festivals and parades were held. Everybody loved just walking down that street.

Because I worked the evening shift at work, every single day I'd walk a few blocks from my bathroom-sized apartment, down that amazing street, to my dad's house. We'd make and eat lunch together. Every day we would sit on his porch while he'd do the newspaper crossword puzzle, and we'd both drink coffee and people watch. I was the only one of my siblings who would tell him absolutely everything, things you wouldn't normally tell your parents. I'd tell him about boys, and he hated that. And I loved that he hated it because I thought it was funny. He didn't really hate it, but it did make him uncomfortable, and it still made me laugh.

I had just turned twenty-one, and like every year for our birthdays, my dad took me out to brunch. We had just gotten back to his house after an incredible meal at this awesome artsy diner that plays the best feel-good blues music. One of my dad's paintings was hanging up for display. The whole topic of discussion was a bit odd. He kept talking about the same thing. When I tried to talk about something different, he'd give a short answer and then come back to this same topic. He'd bring up past decisions I made at all ages growing up that I'd look back on and with a laugh say, "I won't do that again."

As I was about to pull out of his driveway and leave his house after having birthday brunch, my dad said he had something for me upstairs in his apartment and he'd be right back. A birthday present! Though it wasn't wrapped and it wasn't actually intended to be a gift at all, it was one that I will always remember.

It was a stack of papers, big enough to be a college textbook: nicely stapled, three-holed-punched, and carefully highlighted anti-Mormon papers against the Church. I didn't even know he knew about the Mormon Church—not many people did. When we hear of two people in suits knocking on doors we all think of Jehovah's Witnesses. But how did he find out, and why would he have cared? He was the one who taught me acceptance of all, no matter the religion, race, age, or outside appearance. He loved all and was friends with all. But he didn't like how I was a part of something that was so "by the books," and he didn't support what I was now a part of. How ironic that was to me.

Though I was already shocked enough by my "birthday gift," he then threw the stack of papers at me. He wouldn't look me in the eye. I'm not sure I had ever been more shocked by my dad than I was in that exact moment. Then I became shocked at how many different emotions I could feel all at the same time—surprised, confused, upset, hurt, offended.

He was wholeheartedly convinced that if you met elders and you *didn't* get baptized, someone from the Church would come and slit your throat. The thing about contention is that no matter how much you know and no matter how perfectly crafted your response is, people won't listen to you. Contentious situations come from people who won't listen to what you say at all. They aren't having a conversation with you because they want to be educated; they are too busy trying to prove you wrong. And while you are giving your perfectly crafted answer, they aren't listening, just thinking of their next jab toward you.

Except in this situation I didn't have a perfectly crafted answer. I didn't have much of an answer at all, actually, because of how confused I was with what was happening. Regardless, my dad was not up for a discussion. My dad, the most loving and accepting and open man, my best friend and biggest support, looked me right in the eye and said, "Al, I don't want you as a daughter anymore. I don't want you as a daughter anymore. You have to pick. This Church that you *just* found out about, or me—your dad."

Can you imagine hearing that from your dad?

I finally made a connection from our weird conversation at lunch. Somehow he knew that I had been baptized, and he was trying to persuade me to avoid another "I won't do that again" experience to save me the grief or embarrassment.

I remember thinking, *What an easy decision for a difficult situation.*

I already chose who I wanted to follow, didn't I? That decision was made when I was baptized. I already recognized that this happiness I didn't even know existed does! And it only comes from the gospel. I *knew* that. I could physically feel that. I knew that because I went twenty-one years of my life seeing and thinking that it came from somewhere else, and it doesn't. It does not.

So I didn't need time to think about it. I decided right then and there and responded, "I'm sorry. I love you."

You may think that was brave of me to do. Maybe it was, but I didn't feel brave. In reality, I thought it would all blow over. Maybe I just needed to prove a point. Maybe he just needed to prove one to me. My choice would have stayed the same, but maybe it would have been scarier at the time had I known he actually meant it.

After that experience, I would still walk to his house at the same time I always did, and he'd lock the door and never answer. I'd call, and he wouldn't pick up or return my calls. He really kept his word. He would, however, call and speak often to my mom and sisters, which proved to make matters *much* worse. They all had a nice, long chat with my dad about the Church. You know, about the throat-slitting cult I just joined. You could imagine how nervous, mad, confused, and worried they were for me. I got phone calls from everyone, even my mom's coworkers, whom I don't ever remember meeting. There was usually much yelling on their part, and not too much talking on mine. I tried, but I just couldn't get anything said because there was never a space in their sentence for me to butt in. My cheerleader sister Cierra, who always supported me in my spontaneous decisions, was just as much a daddy's girl as I was, so she trusted my dad and listened to him. And so for the first time, and the time I needed it the most, I didn't have my cheerleader.

Being as independent as I am, if they didn't approve of anything else I was doing, it wouldn't have bothered me. With my stubborn independence I never felt like I needed my family's approval on everything I did in my life, because I didn't always get it. Like that one time in high school I pierced my back. My parents obviously both had a fit, and my cheerleader sister may have rolled her eyes at me, but those reactions never lasted. It all blew over that same day. But even if it didn't, it was always over something ultimately insignificant and fleeting in my life, and it didn't matter too much to me how they would react.

But not this time. This wasn't insignificant or fleeting. It was my whole life, and it wasn't blowing over.

Aside from these bizarre things my dad found on the Internet about what we "believe," I think there was a big fear in my family that had nothing do with the things highlighted in that stack of papers thrown at me. I think they had a fear of losing their daughter (or sister or niece or cousin) in the same way I thought I would be losing myself when I first met the elders. I think they had this fear that this church would change me and I would be gone. And it crossed my mind several times that because of those habits I had overcome and they had not, they maybe thought I would judge them or come off that I was better than them or something, which was a heartbreaking thought for me.

Although I did have support from everyone I went to church with, I hardly ever saw any of them outside of church. People drove up to two hours to get to church, so we were spread out. And it didn't help that I worked nights, when everyone was getting home from work and I was just on my way there. I felt incredibly alone. I had never actually felt alone *until* I joined the Church. No noticeable trials came *until* I joined the Church. Life didn't seem hard *until* I joined the Church.

Every time things got hard, *every single second* that I had free I spent reading the Book of Mormon—*every* second I had free. I had a copy of the Book of Mormon everywhere—one in my car, one in my purse, and even one I would sneak into the front of my pants at work, and I would fake bathroom breaks just so I could read for a minute in the bathroom stall. I had a copy wherever I went, just so I could always have it with me in those spare moments throughout my days. I would read it while I was walking and on every single one of my breaks. Not once did my situation change because of it, not really, but every single time I read, I was given the strength and the knowledge to be able to handle what I was going through. That book—*that* is where strength and answers come from. I don't know what I'd do without that book. Scriptures truly do heal a hurting heart and a wounded soul.

All I had were the simple things of the gospel, freshly taught to me by my elders. Sometimes all you have is Heavenly Father, but in everything, that's all you really need. The gospel is not our last option: it's our only option.

I wouldn't have changed anything as I look back at this incredibly hard time. There was *so* much I didn't know about God and *so* much more I didn't know about the gospel. Every day, it took a lot of experimenting on my part to figure out how He works in my life and what He could do for me at a time when it really counted. What would happen if I prayed this way, or asked something like this, or studied like that, or didn't do this? But those blind experiments brought a full, thick, real, and lasting conversion that would help me in every single trial that followed.

"If ye will awake and arouse your faculties, even to an experiment upon my words, and exercise a particle of faith, yea, even if ye can no more than desire to believe, let this desire work in you" (Alma 32:27).

Despite my fear of not saying prayers "correctly," I learned four powerful things: (1.) He hears every prayer, no matter how eloquently they are said. (2.) Nothing is too small or "insignificant" to talk to Him about. I have been really surprised with how quick God is to answer the smallest or silliest of things. (3.) Honesty in our prayers is *crucial* to receive the answers we need. (4.) Listen.

Specific prayers receive specific answers. Heavenly Father answers our prayers, and it is through Him that the right answers and knowledge come. Ask God, not Google. When things were *really* hard, when I didn't like something or understand how it was going to work, or when I felt like giving up, I told Him, "Heavenly Father, this stinks." Or, "This is completely confusing, and I don't agree with this." And even, "Why is this happening? I can't do this, I can't. I'm not this strong, and this is really hard. *Where are you?*"

Sometimes I feel like it's easy to tiptoe around our true feelings and thoughts in fear of maybe offending God or something. Or maybe we don't speak to Him because we're mad at Him because of our circumstances. Regardless of how we feel, tell Him everything. I have found that holding back in prayers not only prevents answers and full conversion but also prevents an intimate, trustworthy, and real relationship with our Father in Heaven.

During this difficult period, these questions plagued my thoughts: How do you teach someone who won't listen? How do you teach someone who you may not get a chance to *speak* to at all? The answer definitely didn't come right away, but it did come: teach by example.

Chapter 5 . . .
NEW LIFE

> To choose happiness is to choose God. And once you choose God, ANYTHING IS POSSIBLE.

AS I ADJUSTED TO this new life, every day was the same. I woke up, and the time I used to spend walking to my dad's house and eating lunch with him now turned into feeding my craving for knowing more and doing better. I became thirsty for knowledge. I couldn't stop reading and studying about the gospel. And when I had to stop, I couldn't stop thinking about it. It was all a selfish pursuit more than anything. I was just chasing happiness. To choose happiness is to choose God. And once you choose God, anything is possible.

I got *Preach My Gospel* as a gift, and I studied out of it *every* day for hours until the pages started falling out from being written on and turned too often. I wanted to make good use of my time, even on the road. I drove with a pocket hymnbook in my hands and glanced down at it while I was driving. I would sing along to these Mormon Tabernacle Choir CDs the elders grew tired of and gave to me because

I wanted so badly to learn the words. I was so eager to learn *anything* I could about the gospel in any degree.

What do you do when you just turned twenty-one, you live in downtown Rochester, NY, where the nightlife is *very* active, and you don't have any friends? Well, I'll tell you what you do. I don't know how many of you have found yourself home alone on a Friday or Saturday night and had those fleeting thoughts of, *I feel lame*. Maybe you didn't; maybe it was just me, because that's how I felt every single Friday and Saturday night. The noise of house parties across the street and all of the many bars just a block over echoed loudly into my bathroom-sized apartment, where I was home alone. And it's not that I missed the nightlife—I didn't. I grew sick of that scene long before I met the elders, and partying was most definitely *not ever* my thing. But it was a clear and consistent reminder that those people at those parties had friends to see and stories to hear and experiences to live. And there I was, sitting home by myself in the middle of my floor, overhearing their laughter. So every Friday and Saturday night I spent on my floor by myself and made up church talks, for fun. Wild, right?

I loved learning more about the Church, and those nights spent on the floor studying and writing talks helped me in more ways than I can count, but it was hard. I hated coming home late at night, driving by the thick of everyone's social life, and walking into an empty apartment. There were too many times I'd drive home crying, absolutely hysterical because I didn't want to be alone. There were plenty of nights I would plead to feel the Spirit, to make things easier, but I didn't. I didn't feel Him at times when I really *needed* to, and I would beg in tears just to feel peace. That happened consistently, and in those moments when I couldn't feel the Spirit, I would think back on the times that I had felt Him, and I held on to that with the little energy I had left.

This didn't make things easy, but it did better equip me to push forward. I read 3 Nephi 13:33: "Seek ye first the kingdom of God and his righteousness, and all these things shall be added unto you." I read it and my whole body started to tingle. It was in that moment I *knew* that no matter what happens, if we put God first, our trials and losses, our lonely times will be made up to us. And it would be not just okay but *better* than what we ever had in mind—better than before the hard times had even started. It was this scripture that I held onto by my fingertips with all the energy I had left, when it felt like I was being pulled by my ankles in the opposite direction. It was this scripture that helped me to use this faith I wasn't sure I had at times. If I wanted to *know* God and not just know *of* Him, the best way to do that wasn't to get mad at Him for what was happening. I had to see what could come from remaining close to Him and holding on to His promises, no matter how dim and distant they seemed.

Ether 6 is a brilliant perspective on those times when we feel like we can't catch our breath, when we catch ourselves asking, "Why? Why me? Why hasn't this passed yet? Where is God, and why hasn't He taken this from me yet?" In Ether 6, Jared and his brother were traveling in barges across the sea. Their journey lasted 344 days—probably much longer than they desired or anticipated. All the while, they were faced with "furious wind" and "great and terrible tempests," many times being completely "buried in the depths of the sea" (verses 5–6). In moments like that, it would have been easy for them to ask, "Why isn't this over yet? Why is this happening when we are following the Lord over to the promised land? God, why won't you deliver us from this long and terrible storm?"

It was consistently so hard for them. The only thing more consistent than their storms, however, was the light. The light that came from the stones to "shine in darkness" (verse 3).

Light that came directly from the Lord. And they made it! They were unharmed and protected, even in the worst of the worst. "When they were buried in the deep there was no water that could hurt them" (verse 7). "No monster of the sea could break them, neither whale that could mar them; and they did have *light continually*, whether it was above the water or under the water" (verse 10; emphasis added).

It was the Lord God, *not* Satan, who caused those furious winds to blow toward the promised land. Not once were they left alone. And though the storm seemed to be preventing them from progressing, it was actually helping them travel toward the place they needed to go—the promised land. Through all of that, they were always moving *forward*, always guided by God, and always having light. "The wind did never cease to blow towards the promised land" (verse 8). How easy it would have been to murmur and be upset at God. But when they finally arrived, they were not mad at God or upset by the storms from their journey but were filled with gratitude! Immediately when they reached land, the first thing they did was give thanks (verse 12). They left behind so much to go to new territory, acting just on faith. Yes, it was hard and probably incredibly scary, but when they got there, things were much *better* than where they were before, regardless of the comforts they left behind and the trials they endured. After all they went through, they chose to give thanks. All of their discomfort didn't matter; all their suffering was completely replaced with happiness, with gratitude. Because they made it. Because it was better than what they knew was available for themselves and greater than they even knew existed. That's how it will always be with God. That's the promise He has given to us, the promise we must never lose sight of: we will make it, and everything will be not just all right but *better*.

In all of the discouragement you may feel now—all of your sorrow, sadness, loneliness, darkness, and "storms" of life you may be traveling through right now—look to this story. Look to the light you *do* have, even if it seems as small as a stone. Look to the Lord. Look for His hand, even when you feel buried under the waves of mortality. He is always there with you, always guiding you. It's beautiful. We need to trust that everything God does is to help us receive greater blessings in life. When you are trying to do what God will have you do, know that those hard times *are* moving you closer to where He needs you to be. Our trials move us closer to where things are greater than they ever could have been before. Your stormy journey may be taking much longer than you desire or feel you have strength to endure, but do not let discouragement stop you from trying and turning to Him. Hard times *will* consistently be there—that won't change—but so will Christ. And with Him we are able to overcome and conquer absolutely everything—every feeling of loneliness, discomfort, weakness, sadness, and temptation. Do not let your trials dictate and alter your perception of truths and promises given. Hold on to what you know; it will be your anchor in the storms. He will never give up on you. Do not give up on Him.

"Mine eyes are upon you, and the heavens and the earth are in mine hands, and the riches of eternity are mine to give. Ye endeavored to believe that ye should receive the blessing which was offered unto you; but behold, verily I say unto you there were fears in your hearts, and verily this is the reason that ye did not receive" (D&C 67:2–3).

Fear not. Forget not whose hands you're in. You are not left alone or forgotten. You are not being punished. You *are* being led. You are being guided and directed. You are protected. You will make it. And it will be greater than you could even imagined.

"Fear not, little children, for you are mine" (D&C 50:41).

Chapter 6 . . .

TRIALS & ANDY'S BAPTISM

> No matter who we are or what we're going through, there is always a solution. It is and always will be Christ. The gospel is not our last option; IT IS OUR ONLY OPTION.

IF I WANTED TO feel happiness, I knew I needed to stay as close to the Lord and His gospel as I could. I didn't have such hard times until I established a relationship with my God and joined His Church, but I also never felt that real and physical happiness before either. I knew that if I wanted to keep that and feel that, I needed to do everything I could to stay close to Him. I couldn't let anything get in the way, especially my trials. It definitely seems easy when I write that decision down in a single sentence. But with my trials of loneliness on top of everything else, I had to make that decision to keep going a daily thing. Every day I had to remake the decision to put God first, and sometimes I'd have to make that decision several times a day.

In the middle of all this, I got a MySpace message from, we'll call him Andy, this guy I went to high school with, wanting to get in touch with me and catch up. *How bizarre*, I thought. I was never friends with him, and his crowd was most definitely not my crowd. Why now would he want to hang out with me almost four years after school? As bizarre as it seemed, I felt a pull toward the invite.

We went out to ride go-karts. He picked me up, and without hesitation the first thing out of my mouth, almost unconsciously, was, "The Catholic Church isn't true." How awkward for him, I'm sure. I had a complete word vomit and just rambled on about all the unanswered questions the world as a whole had. We had grown up going to the same church, but he wasn't religious. And I am confident he had no intention of becoming so now or even indulging in religious conversation. I'm sure it was definitely unlike any hangout he's had and not what he had in mind. He actually wanted to invite me to play on his indoor soccer team; they needed a girl on their team or else they had to play down a man. I'm surprised the invite was still there after the way our day had gone. I said I only would if I could teach him a lesson about the gospel before each game. Surprisingly, he agreed.

He didn't agree because he was interested in learning more, and he definitely didn't keep hanging out with me because of our commonalities, because there weren't many. But it was just like me wanting to see the elders every day. We are all born with the Light of Christ; every single one of us has it. But when we receive the gift of the Holy Ghost, the promise that it is ours to keep and have always is *very* real. Oftentimes we as members don't recognize His presence because of its consistency in our life. We navigate through life so comfortably, relying upon it without even realizing it sometimes. But when you do not have that gift, you can see and feel it in others. We become like bugs to a lightbulb, and we're drawn in by the light and don't want to leave. That's what was happening to Andy, being pulled toward the light.

It was still really hard in my family, and no one was speaking to me (and how heartbreaking it was to see my family go through hard things that could have easily been avoided if they had the gospel). But here Andy was, and he knew what I was a part of and still wanted to hang out with me. I couldn't bear the thought of passing up any opportunity to share what I had with anyone I could. I became sick at the thought of people not having what I had, of people going through life without help, without guidance, without prayer, without God, without *real* happiness. Choosing God is choosing happiness. I was going to tell every single person I came in contact with about what I had and what they could have too. Besides, I made a promise to God when I got baptized that I would do everything I could to help.

I taped pass-along cards on all my doors and windows and my mailbox. I had a bumper sticker on the back of my car, saying, "Mormon.org," complemented with a gold Angel Moroni figurine that I glued to the dash of my car. I'd wear shirts that said "Mormon" on them in hopes to intrigue conversation even during the menial errands I had to run.

Every day before work I would go out with the elders and help them teach investigators and less actives members, including Andy and my sister Rachel, who came to my baptism with Scott.

I never would have imagined my own sister would start to take the lessons from missionaries. But then again, a set of elders—not the ones teaching me—saw me my first day of church, and they later confessed to me that they both turned to each other and said I was the last person they thought would ever get baptized and they would never see me there again. One of them even wrote it in his journals and confessed it to me at my baptism. I didn't blame him. I thought I was the last one to ever become religious too, and we know how that turned out. I have learned that it's not up to us to pick and choose who we think is ready to hear the gospel.

Conversion is the most intimate thing we can witness and experience. There is nothing more personal than the invitation to learn about and join this gospel because it is an invitation to change everything. Experiencing it for ourselves and witnessing it in someone else is completely different. I was changing without even recognizing it at first. I was making decisions to do and not do things without exactly knowing why. Overcoming bad habits and relearning and changing my whole mindset was a complete reconstruction of myself, and it seemed so long and out of nowhere at the same time.

Seeing it in Andy it seemed so obvious. He cancelled his gambling bank account after the first lesson with the elders and had no idea why. I did, though—it was the Spirit. It was his soul flying after the gospel like a bug to a light.

We went to the Church history sites in Palmyra and watched the Joseph Smith movie they had playing in the visitor center. I have a deep, deep love for this film, and just thinking about this movie brings me the Spirit so overwhelmingly. While I was watching it this time around, I couldn't help but wonder what Andy was thinking. That's all I could think about. When it ended, we stood up, laughed at each other because the elders and I were all crying, and after minutes of talking, noticed Andy was still sitting there. He hadn't moved an inch and wasn't even blinking.

"I didn't know it was going to be that kind of movie," he eventually stuttered.

I'll never forget those words. He stood up and pushed through us to the other room of the visitor center to where there was a huge picture of Thomas S. Monson. He stood in front of it and just stared for minutes with no movement, no blinking. And then it happened, the most intimate thing. Everything clicked, and I saw it happen. I saw a before and after happen in front of my eyes where the gospel just clicked. He hadn't a clue exactly what was happening, but I did. It happened the same way with me. And it happened the same way with Scott *and* my oldest sister, Rachel.

It turned out that Scott, the only one I invited to my baptism, was a member of the Church, except he had stopped going when he was just barely a teenager, and at that point he was in his thirties. He thought the same way I used to think, that he didn't need help from anyone or anything, and he definitely didn't need religion. But because of my awkward sort-of invitation to come to my baptism, he once again felt the Spirit that he'd been long passed due of feeling. His desire to learn more and do better intrigued my oldest sister to learn more. Despite her thick pagan beliefs (which my dad fully supported), and even though she was the last person I thought would be baptized—aside from myself—Rachel and Scott gained a testimony the same way Andy and I did: through everyday efforts with the simple principles of the gospel.

When you finally know the gospel is true, you become overwhelmed. You have racing thoughts of fear of what this could mean for your life now and how unexpected and scary whatever the next steps are going to be. Knowing that God is real and the gospel is true is another way of saying your life will never be the same. It will be better, yes, but that change is still extremely scary when you have such a long history and contrast of life filled with decisions, plans, and dreams completely out of sorts with the Lord's will.

With Andy and Rachel, the adversary quickly stepped in, and they both battled with the idea of getting baptized for weeks. You'll be surprised by everything that comes up to prevent a baptism from happening; it's wild. Your thoughts go crazy, and the adversary gets creative.

Andy, too, lost his friends, and he had to deal with the reoccurring threat from his dad of committing suicide at the cost of Andy's membership in the Church. Rachel had succumbed to my same position and had lost the support from the rest of our family. Although she always had support from her friends, seeing the pain it brought our other sister and losing contact with our dad left a big enough wound to hold her back from stepping into the waters of baptism for much longer than she had first decided. I'd regularly get phone calls from her saying she knew it was true but she couldn't follow through because she couldn't bear to bring that much anguish to the rest of our family. It hurt my heart to hear that.

But darkness cannot exist where there is light. Constant effort to increase your light is crucial *after* you receive a witness or answer of any kind to drive out that darkness. It's crucial because darkness can be found everywhere and pops up and presents itself in the most unexpected ways. The one thing Heavenly Father and Satan have in common is that they both desire to have us.

But the truth is that our trials and our circumstances will never alter the unchanging truth that this is all real. That no matter who we are or what we're going through, there is always a solution. It is and always will be Christ. The gospel is not our last option; it is our only option. It's how and why we are here. Giving up is not an option, and it never can be. No matter how hard things get and how easy it would be to give up and go back to where things made sense and were comfortable, it cannot change the fact that this is real. He is real. His promises are real. And this happiness is real. And our forever depends upon how we choose to act today.

"Know ye not that ye are in the hands of God? Know ye not that he hath all power?" (Mormon 5:23).

Know ye not that He will *not* leave you and He will not stop trying? Know ye not that He misses you and wants you back? If we think our Father in Heaven would do anything to prevent us from returning to Him and being happy *now,* we're wrong.

Andy got baptized and became a great support to me, and Scott became worthy to baptize my sister Rachel. Truly, the best thing we can do for ourselves and for our family is to obey God.

Chapter 7 . . .

PREPARING TO MOVE

> Sure, our future is uncertain
> at times, but how exciting that is!
> How exciting to know that it is
> LED AND GUIDED BY GOD!

THOUGH IT WAS EXCITING to have one of my sisters join the Church, the hard times got much harder. Loneliness was still in full gear for me because I still had that awful evening shift at work that kept me from any in-person support. And my dad didn't seem to react well now that he had "lost" two of his three daughters to this "cult." My sister unfortunately lived next to my dad's girlfriend's house (and by "girlfriend" I mean they have been together for over ten years; my dad is just against marriage). My sister could not escape the daily and contentious bashes against her, loud diatribes that were *only* shouted when my dad's girlfriend knew my sister was outside in her backyard. We could hear her yell often about how awful we were and how we didn't deserve a dad. And still, even though my dad was next door, he never spoke to us.

To cope with the hard times, I selfishly chased happiness for myself by going out to help teach with the elders every day. Me chasing after happiness was simply doing anything gospel related. I loved seeing that change in other people—how personal and individual Heavenly Father was with us. Missionary work became like my hiding spot from the adversary. Then it hit me.

"Oh my heck, Heavenly Father, I want to go on a mission!"

I *knew* my answer was going to be yes. I knew it. That is a righteous, good thing to want to do, so why be denied a good thing, right? Do you know what my answer was?

Move to Utah.

Uh, that's not what I asked for. I didn't want to move to Utah. I honestly completely forgot Utah was even a state until I met all these elders. I thought maybe if I asked differently, I would get a different answer, but that was not the case. Maybe if I explained to Him how much it meant to me to let me do this, how important it was, He would change His mind. But that was not what happened.

My answer came as a reoccurring thought, one I figured if I ignored long enough would go away. It didn't. Weeks and weeks had passed, and it kept coming back. But what it came down to was this: I just found out that God *is* real. Not only that, but He in reality speaks to us. He does. Who would I be if I said, "Hey God, you're wrong." I can't do that, because He's God! What would I be if I said that to God? And how guilty I would have felt if I finally got an answer and didn't do anything about it. The guilt would have killed me. So finally I said to Him in prayer, "Fine, I'll go, but I'm not happy about it. Just so you know."

That was incredibly difficult for many reasons. It's hard to know your desires are not His will. But it's not about picking what we want to do and just asking for Heavenly Father's help with it; it is about doing what He asks of us and receiving those blessings, help, and comfort to follow through with *His* will.

No matter how many times I prayed and asked, no matter how many times I literally begged and *pleaded* to know *why* I needed to move to Utah, Heavenly Father would not answer me that. That was incredibly frustrating and difficult. It's hard enough to do something you completely dread, but it's even harder when you don't know the reason behind it. What was I supposed to tell my family? What was I suppose to tell my dad?

When my dad found out I was moving across the country, I heard from him for the first time in months. He said, "Al, why are you leaving us? Why are you moving all the way across the country where you don't know a single person? Why? This church is tearing our family apart!"

And what was I suppose to say? My dad is not a religious man; I couldn't say, "Hey Dad, God told me to, so . . ." He wouldn't have understood that. How hard that was, to see him so mad, and offended, and confused, and worried, and sad. And I couldn't comfort him in any way because I didn't have a logical answer to give him. And I didn't even have that answer for myself, to comfort myself.

Every week, I was so excited for Sundays. I craved Sundays. It wasn't often I saw other members during the week. They lived so far away; we were so spread out, and I worked evenings when everyone was just getting out of work or school. Sundays were the only time I had to see other members. Our church building was in an old post office. It was pretty small, with fold-up chairs instead of pews. And it was the greatest building! The feelings of familiarity and comfort in that old post office brought me so much needed strength just from walking through the doors. I was excited because they understood how prayer worked, and they understood the Spirit. I just so badly wanted someone to support me in my decision to move. "Al, let me know if you need help with anything," or even, "Al, that's interesting." I would have even accepted that. But for the most part, they all said the same thing, even my branch president:

"Al, don't move to Utah. If you move to Utah, no one will like you. If you go there, you will *not* fit in. Don't do it, Al. Don't go."

They thought I was naïve—getting baptized and then moving to Utah. Hearing that from everyone left me a pool of different feelings: mad, unmotivated, angry, offended, confused. I was scared to death and doubtful that it was an actual answer from God. But nonetheless, I kept going regardless—mostly experimenting with God, I suppose. The only way to fully learn and know about Heavenly Father was to try new things and figure out how He worked in my life.

"Now when our hearts were depressed, and we were about to turn back, behold, the Lord comforted us, and said: Go" (Alma 26:27).

Because of my prayers, there was a time frame in which I knew I needed to move. I had a two-month window to prepare, find a job, or find a place to live. Every day I would try to find *something* to work out, *anywhere* in the state of Utah, because Heavenly Father didn't tell me where in Utah to move. He just said, "That state—go."

So I said, "Oh, okay, Google Maps and prayer, we'll just figure it out!"

Everyday in my free time I would search for something—anything—in that state. And it wasn't as easy as hopping on my laptop in the comfort of my own home; Internet was expensive. I had to travel downtown to the public library and pay to use theirs. Every day I would try, for two whole months, and nothing fell into place. You know how time just sort of slows down when things are hard? Two months is a good chunk of time, but it honestly felt like two years. I tried every day and had *nothing*. It was incredibly exhausting.

There were two days before I was supposed to move, and I had nothing to show for my efforts. I had already given my two weeks notice to my job weeks ago, and someone was moving into my bathroom-sized apartment in those two days. If this didn't work out, I would be broke and homeless, so you could imagine how nervous I was. If this was His idea, why was nothing working? I was confused. I was tired. I was drained. My body physically hurt because of how exhausted I was from trying. And I was mad. I was mad at God.

I found myself on the floor screaming at Heavenly Father, "I don't know what else to do! I don't know what else to do; I'm praying, I'm reading, I'm fasting—I don't know how many times—and I have nothing to show for it. *Why?* Why is something so right so hard? Do you still even care about *me?* Are you even listening to me? Are you even there at all?"

I spent that night just hysterical on my floor because I put so much into this, and I felt like I was getting nothing back from God, even though I was doing something He wanted me to! Hope was fading, and I was too tired, too exhausted, too worn out, and too tried to want to think about faith. I thought I was faithful enough during those two months. Why wasn't this over yet? Why hadn't this worked out?

CHAPTER 7

Hours passed, and I was still screaming at Him. For hours I pled for an answer of why I needed to keep going, *why*, and never received an answer.

Comfort did come, but not until I lost my voice from yelling at God, until I couldn't even speak anymore and no tears were left to cry, even though I wished there were. It wasn't until then, when I closed my mouth and *listened*, that I received, that I heard what God had to say to me. The Spirit always speaks, but it is up to us to actually listen and not just listen for what we want to hear.

And in that moment, I thought of Christ. I thought of the time He fed the multitude and when He raised Lazarus from the dead. I said out loud, "Holy cow, those are great miracles!" And while waving my hand up at Heavenly Father, I yelled, "That is what I need, a miracle!" And I thought, *What happened right before those miracles came? Well, Christ prayed, right? But they were prayers of gratitude.* And I thought, *Wow, what an incredible example.* Not only did Christ know Heavenly Father was in fact there, but He also was aware of what He needed. And Christ, He had such great faith—perfect faith—that He didn't even ask for help but instead gave thanks before knowing that Heavenly Father would bless Him. It's easy to feel like we have enough faith to receive blessings and miracles *now* and that answers really can come in the exact second we want them. But sometimes the true test of faith is waiting for blessings to come when you have faith that they will come quickly.

So in that moment, when I needed to ask Him for so much, I didn't ask Him for a single thing. That was hard. It was hard because I needed to force myself to use this faith I didn't think I had in the moment. It was one of those prayers where you fall asleep at the end, or maybe even in the middle; all you know is that it's the next day.

"Your Father knoweth what things ye have need of, before ye ask him" (Matthew 6:8).

I woke up to my phone ringing. At that point I was leaving the very next day, and I still had nothing. The phone call was from this lady I didn't remember ever calling. "Hi!" she said, almost too cheerfully for me. "I just checked my voicemail, and I have one from you two months ago. Do you still need a place to live? Because I have one for you."

What? Was this a joke? Holy cow. Talk about an eleventh-hour blessing, literally. An eleventh-hour blessing and a lot of gray hair I got from it. As soon as everything did work out, my first thought was, *Duh. Of course it would.* Just because it didn't happen in my time frame, the way I had in mind, didn't mean it wasn't going to happen. Everything I was thinking and feeling—doubt, concern, worry, anger, confusion, frustration—was just showing my lack of faith, right? And that's not how we're blessed. As soon as it worked out, I just said to Heavenly Father, "I'm sorry."

It made me think of the First Vision. Right before I moved, I drove to Palmyra one last time on my own, just to bury myself deep in the Sacred Grove and ponder. I found a wooden bench to sit on, and I read the First Vision.

"Exerting all my powers to call upon God to deliver me out of the power of this enemy which had seized upon me, and at the very moment when I was ready to sink into despair and abandon myself to destruction—not to an imaginary ruin, but to the power of some actual being from the unseen world, who had such marvelous power as I had never before felt in any being—just at this moment of great alarm, I saw a pillar of light exactly over my head" (Joseph Smith—History 1:16).

At the *very moment* Joseph was ready to sink into despair, at the *very moment* of great alarm, Christ came. Christ came *before* it was too late, at the perfect time. Just like when

Peter was walking on water, Christ came and grabbed him and helped him before he fully sank. And so it is with us, and so it will be every time with Him. Christ is always there for us, and He *will* help and deliver us before it is ever too late.

Do not worry over things you have no control over. Refrain always from thinking you are alone or that your prayers aren't heard. Refrain from thinking that He doesn't care or that you will be shortchanged from the absolute best. Sure, our future is uncertain at times, but how exciting that is! How exciting to know that it is led and guided by God! Do not let time and trials dim your faith or diminish the truthfulness of His promises to you. His promises are so real, and they never expire. Never lose confidence. Trust your companion, the Spirit, who works not just with you but in you, and always keep going.

Chapter 8 . . .

LEAVING EVERYTHING

> We need to TRUST
> that everything GOD does
> is to help us succeed.

SO, I MOVED TO UTAH, and that was wild, absolutely wild to me! I had to fit my whole entire life into a two-door Alero Oldsmobile, which isn't much of a life if you think of the size of a two-door car made in the 1990s, especially since I brought along my dog, Lucas. He's a discount dog, so I don't fully know what kind of dog he is. But I made room for all eighty pounds' worth of discount dog in my car with the rest of my stuff, which wasn't much. It was interesting to see the things I took with me, but it was even more interesting to see the things I left behind.

Think of all your things, everything in your room and in your home—all your knickknacks, furniture, DVDs, everything—and picture it all on the side of the road for the garbage man to pick up. That's how it was for me. Other than my clothes, all I took with me and all I could fit was my journals and Church books. And I laughed and thought, *How did my life get to where it is right now?*

Moving wasn't like a mission or school where you have the idea that you could eventually, one day, maybe end up back home. I was going, and I was going to stay. As far as I knew at the time, I would be in Utah for the rest of my life.

I was leaving behind my branch. I loved that branch! When I am older and think back to my "childhood memories" of the Church, they will be there, at the branch. They will be the people and the examples, the experiences, and the lessons I had while in that old post office building. It was home.

I was leaving behind the only way of living that I knew.

I was leaving behind my family, my dad. Luckily I was able to say good-bye to him, but it was one of the hardest things I've ever done in my life. I gave him a hug good-bye, and he was crying. I have only seen my dad cry once, and that was when I was in the third grade and he told me and my sisters he was moving out. But he was crying now. He was about to say something to me but stopped himself. As I pulled out of his driveway, he walked and followed the car until it met the road, and he stood there, crying, and waved. It was then that I realized I'd have to cope with the idea that I may never see my dad ever again. The image of him standing at the end of his driveway crying as I pulled away left me with an incredibly heavy heart.

I drove to my mom's house, where my sisters were. Things started to turn around a little bit between them, and it was awful that I was leaving them right when things were getting better and we were making progress. My mom agreed to have the missionaries over for dinner and a lesson my last day in New York. She lived on her own and loved the idea of being able to cook for more people, but she mostly loved the idea that she was doing something to make me happy before I left.

Though, for the record, my mom never struggled with it like my dad did. Her feelings toward my membership in the Church changed consistently, usually depending on who she spoke to that day. And there were plenty of angry phone calls from her saying, "I can't believe you lied to me and you do (insert any crazy-weird throat-slitting antic here)." But for the most part it didn't take long for her to realize that after my baptism, regardless of whatever I seemed to be a part of, I wanted to spend more time with her, and I became more patient and loving and fun and positive. And what mom wouldn't eat that up?

My sister Cierra was once again my cheerleader and surprised me with a tattoo she got of the outline of Utah on her arm with a heart in it. My other sister, Rachel, came by to say good-bye too. My mom brought a twin-size mattress up from the basement and laid it on the floor in her front room for me to sleep on. Since I had already moved out of my bathroom-sized apartment, I was going to sleep there for a few hours and then be on my way at 3:00 a.m. All four of us squeezed onto the twin-size mattress and cuddled and told funny stories about each other when we were growing up. The night was a perfect balance of laughter and sadness. It was like a scene from the movies.

I fell asleep to my mom's and sisters' laughter.

Andy came late that night about the same time I had set my alarm to wake up and leave. When I had told him God told me to move, he decided he wanted to come and move too. He wanted a bigger support group now that he was also freshly baptized and had lost his family's and friends' support. It was comforting to know that I'd have someone just a car in front of me to drive across the country with, especially since he had mapped out the whole trip and all I'd have to do was follow him.

My phone alarm went off at 2:30 a.m., and I woke up alone in the front room. I'm not sure how much sleep I actually got because of my nerves, but it was enough to have missed being able to say a formal good-bye to my sisters. But I couldn't have thought of a better good-bye than hearing them laugh. When I sat up, I saw Andy standing in the room, staring at me.

"Were you able to sleep at all?" I asked.

No answer.

"Did you rest? Are you ready to go?"

No answer.

The way he was staring at me made me nervous, and my heart beat fast. I was so afraid to ask my next question, but I had to: "Are you still coming?"

His eyes got teary, and I knew my answer. He wasn't. My mind started racing, my heart was coming out of my chest, and I started to panic. How could he ditch me? He had no apartment to go back to, and his car was completely packed. All he had left to do was just leave; that's it. I wasn't prepared to do this on my own. My mind and heart weren't prepared to do this by myself. My stomach knotted, and I became so nauseous.

Andy started explaining about how he was moving for the wrong reasons, but my mind was so busy trying to figure out what my first step was that I didn't listen to him. Step one: don't tell my mom. I didn't dare tell my mom I was making the cross-country trip by myself and put her through all that worry.

Walking out the door in complete shock, I was surprised to see my mom awake, standing there in her bathrobe, half asleep, waiting to say good-bye to me. She hugged Andy much tighter than she hugged me and told him, "Don't ever leave her. Promise me."

He promised. But we both knew he was going to leave me about three steps out the door. I got in my car, and I was so scared and upset that I literally forgot how to turn it on. *How am I supposed to do this by myself?* Just as before, the Spirit always speaks, but it is up to us to listen. It was in the quiet moment of my panic and hyperventilating that I realized I wasn't alone. I never have been.

"And I was led by the Spirit, not knowing beforehand the things which I should do. Nevertheless I went forth" (1 Nephi 4:6–7). Not once did the thought come into my mind to not go or to postpone the trip. I knew that wasn't what Heavenly Father wanted me to do. I knew there were far better things to come than anything I would leave behind, because everything God does is to help us succeed. Embrace the future; embrace the unexpected, knowing who is guiding you. Sacrifice is *never* a bad thing if we have a testimony.

I was still terrified even though I knew it was right. I didn't know what my first step was going to be. I had no idea where I was going because Andy did all the planning. I wasn't even sure if I was to take a right or a left out of my mom's driveway. I cried and hyperventilated all the way to the Pennsylvania border. My mind was still racing and my body shaking because of how unprepared I felt with this cross-country move. Because of my independence, had it had been under any other circumstance, this might have been really great and exciting. But doing it against my will and cannonballing into it alone and blindly it was not the recipe for either of those feelings.

I drove twelve hours until I made it to Chicago, where there was a hotel room that Andy already paid for a few weeks ago. I tried to eat, but I couldn't. My body was freaking out too much to eat. It wasn't until I looked out the window that I realized I didn't recognize a single thing. It was then I found myself absolutely and completely and *physically* consumed with all of this fear and doubt and anxiety. I was completely consumed with loneliness. I had never felt more alone than I did in that moment. It was so captivating and powerful that it brought me to the floor of the hotel room, hysterical. My body hurt from this overwhelming physical force, and the only thing I could do was lie on that floor in the middle of downtown Chicago and cry so hard that my throat hurt from trying to catch my breath. I started screaming at God, "I can't do this! I can't! You have the wrong person. I'm not this strong! I'm not."

How badly I wanted to turn back to where things made sense and where things were comfortable. How badly I wanted to be laughing with my mom and sisters and hugging my dad again. *Why* did I have to leave when things were starting to get better?

I was pleading for an answer: Why did I need to keep going? Why did I need to leave? I put every bit of energy and faith I had into that plea, and Heavenly Father still did not give me an answer. The temptation to turn around, to quit, to go back to where things were comfortable and where things made sense was through the roof. This time I knew what to do to get rid of those feelings: "Al, shut your mouth. *Listen.*"

My eyes were closed, and my body exhausted. I tried to stop my panicked thoughts so the only thing I could hear was my deep breaths and the Spirit. It was then, when I was seeking and listening, that I saw Him. I saw Christ.

I want you to picture this (and actually do it). Picture Christ standing right in front of you. Picture what He looks like to you.

And then, He smiles.

He smiles at *you*.

While my red, puffy, heavy eyes were closed, I saw Christ standing right in front of me, looking at me. And then, He smiled. He smiled at *me*. That was it. That was all I needed. I *knew* that no matter how hard things were, no matter how much I didn't understand, I *knew* that He was happy with what I was doing. That it was right.

I cannot think of a greater feeling than the Lord's approval of what you're doing. His approval is so powerful it can trump every negative feeling you have.

I made a promise to myself that day. It was a promise I meant literally at the time, but it's a promise I try to keep spiritually every single day: I have to keep going. I can't stop. I can't even take a break. Because the moment you stop, the moment you take a break, *that* is when fear, doubt, anxiety, loneliness, and temptation creep in. I knew that if I stopped, if I even took a break, I would end up in a direction Heavenly Father would not want me to go. At the time it was probably back home to New York, but spiritually—I think you know where I'm going with that. So I said, "Okay, I'm going. I'm going, and I'm not stopping. I can't." And I didn't. I literally did not stop. I didn't take a break. I left a note on the bed of the hotel room that said, "Visit Mormon.org," with a happy face, and then I drove over twenty-two hours straight from Chicago all the way to Utah Valley, Utah. I didn't stop to eat, not even at a drive-thru. I couldn't. You know, I'd stop to get gas, but I'd yell at my dog, Lucas, "Go to the bathroom on this gas pump because when this tank is full, we're going!"

It was the most uncomfortable drive you could ever imagine. I was driving in the dead of summer, and my car's AC was broken. My driver's side window would not roll down, and my cruise control didn't work. And I had an eighty-pound dog breathing. On. My. Face. It was terrible.

Twenty-two hours in a car is a very long time. My legs were not there anymore. They were gone, just completely detached from my body. My body was twitching, and not just little twitches here and there. My body was doing things your body should not be doing. I heard this weird and consistent buzzing in my ear, and I could see black spots everywhere. I had gone so long without eating, moving, and communicating that I couldn't even form real sentences in my head. And I had seen too many movies that made me terrified of pulling over for a power nap, afraid of my gas being siphoned out of my car or being chased by some masked guy with a chain saw. But I was more afraid of someone stealing my gas than coming at me with a chain saw because I was broke. One of the only phone calls I got was from Andy's mom. They couldn't find Andy, and they called the cops. His parents and the cops told me that I had completely ruined their family and that him being brainwashed and missing was all my fault.

The other phone call was from Gary. I didn't exactly know who Gary was, but I briefly met him a few weeks previously when he was visiting my singles branch. He and his son were from Utah and were visiting to see the Palmyra sites before his son left on a mission. Gary overheard that I was planning a move to his state and asked for my number. I didn't think he'd actually remember or call. But he did. He is such a happy and caring man, and his genuine happiness and excitement and willingness toward me, without even knowing me, became strength for me while on the road. If Gary knew that I'd make it there in one piece, then surely I could believe that too.

I had never seen a mountain before I was driving from Wyoming to Utah and drove through Provo Canyon, but I still couldn't see a mountain because it was dark. I could tell something very tall was on each side of me. So while my body was shutting down—legs unattached, body twitching, heavy eyes seeing large black spots, ears buzzing—I started to come down this windy canyon where the edge of the road had a drop-off right to the center of the earth. Then I see an avalanche sign. Then a falling-rock sign. Then an elk sign. I remember thinking, *WHERE AM I?*

I got in at about 3:00 a.m. and ended up staying in a spare room at Gary's house. With my body shutting down and my eyes barely opened, I didn't dare try to figure out the streets' coordinate system to find my house.

But as soon as I woke up, I was so excited to see my new home. I *knew* that Heavenly Father prepared something so great for me because of how hard it was. He's the one who wanted me to do this in the first place; this was His idea. I knew that as soon as I got my new home where God had led me, all these answers and excitement would come, and everything would make sense and be great. I went to the backyard where my entrance was, my heart beating fast out of excitement, and I thought, *This is it! This is where He wants me to be.* I saw that the grass was up past my hips. It was very tall and very dead. And all these old, broken toys and rusted treasures were braided into the grass. I don't know what it was—actually I'm really grateful I don't know what it was—but something smelled so bad. It was terrible. And there were a few kids with no clothes on playing in the yard.

I told Heavenly Father, "Really, this is it? This is where you brought me? *Neat.*"

I'm not sure what happened to my blankets, but they somehow didn't make it into my car. The first few nights, I actually slept on the floor, wrapped in a towel (and it would be over a month before I was able to buy a used mattress). The line in 1 Nephi "My father dwelt in a tent" (2:15) never had as much meaning to me as it did then. Lehi left everything—his home, his friends, his riches—to follow the Lord. Leaving behind everything he had, he found himself in the middle of nowhere in a tent, with nothing but his murmuring family and his faith.

"We have been driven out of the land of our inheritance; but we have been led to a better land" (2 Nephi 10:20). Though a smelly jungle backyard didn't seem like a "better land" to me in any way, I just needed to trust that everything God does is to help us succeed.

Chapter 9 . . .

UTAH

GOD IS FOR US, so it doesn't matter who is against us.

SO THERE I WAS, my very first day in Utah! There I was in action of where God told me to be, but what was I supposed to do now? I hadn't the slightest idea. Heavenly Father still wouldn't answer me that yet. I ended up driving down State Street, mainly because it was the only street I could find and it stretched through every city of the valley. My mind was racing with so many thoughts. A new thought was coming before I even finished my previous thought: "I can't believe I just did that. I can't believe I'm doing this. I have no idea where I'm going. Holy cow! It is so clean here. I could eat off these sidewalks. You don't want to do that in New York. Oh my gosh! These mountains are huge! I have never seen a mountain before, and they are huge!"

I was driving along, thinking so many things, my mind going a mile a second, and then I saw it. I saw the most beautiful thing I have ever seen.

Café Rio.

We don't have those in New York, and you have to know that tacos, they're a thing. Tacos are one of those things that once I start eating, I don't know when to stop. So I'm driving and thinking all these things: "I don't know where I'm going. It's really clean. These mountains are HUGE, and OH MY GOSH! TACOS!"

I made a U-turn.

This is a story you have to picture. You know how the line kind of snakes around so that when you're waiting, you're waiting in a big group of people? Okay, so there I was, right in the middle of this big group of people. I was really tense. You know how you can tell when someone's staring at you from behind? You can just *feel* it. It's like lasers. That was how I felt, except these lasers were everywhere and from every direction. I was standing there, holding a Church book with both arms on my chest, kind of hugging it. It was a biography on one of the prophets. I felt like I was under a ton of pressure. When you can feel those lasers, your body just sort of tightens up, and it's all you can focus on. Those were ten of the longest minutes of my life, and the guy next to me finally got my attention. He lightly tapped my arm and said with a smug tone and look on his face, "You know, it's pretty ironic, you holding *that* book looking the way *you* do."

My heart broke. Stomach knotted. Eyes teared up.

That was the first thing said to me when I moved here. Immediately I thought of everyone back home saying, "Al, don't go. Don't move there. You will *not* fit in. *No one* will like you."

It took a bit for me to react. So many emotions ran through me, and I had to decide which one I was going to express to him. What I so badly wanted to do was to turn to him and yell and cry to him, "Do you know what I just went through?! Do you know how hard this is? Do you know what and *who* I had to give up to be here? And I don't even know why!"

I so badly wanted to just walk around everywhere with my scriptures so that the lasers would stop, but they didn't. I craved more than anything for people to just know that I was *trying*. That's it. I was *trying*. But they didn't know just by looking at me. It hurt me so badly that it became physically exhausting. What bothered me most was that I was judged for who I used to be and not who I was becoming. For whatever reason, no one ever considered that I hadn't grown up in the Church. They always assumed I was rebelling against God. Regardless, no one should be treated that way, no matter what their journey is.

Normally, I felt like I could easily go up to anyone and hug them and say, "Hi! I'm Al, and we're going to be great friends," and mean it. That's just who I was. It's just what I did. I could talk to anyone anytime about anything, no problem. But other than that man in Café Rio, no one spoke to me. I would be at grocery stores and people would turn around and walk the other way, pull their kids in closer to them, or just stare at me, looking either terrified or disgusted. Daily experiences like that made it so incredibly hard to want to approach other people on my own.

Guys my age were looking for temple-worthy girls (guys, you better have that goal!), but I didn't exactly look temple worthy. They didn't even speak to me. It was the first time it ever occurred to me that, appearance aside, knowing about my lifestyle before joining the Church could stop guys from wanting to not just date but even befriend me. That was really hard, being in a new place, not knowing anyone, not knowing why I was there or what to do, and feeling absolutely, completely, and utterly alone and "cast out."

CHAPTER 9

This was what I left home for? This was what I sacrificed so much to be brought to?

The feelings of loneliness were absolutely through the roof. I was by myself, all the way across the country with no one. I was still begging with all my energy to know why I needed to keep going, why I needed to be there, and I still did not get an answer. I never felt alone until I joined the Church, and I sometimes felt as though I was missing out on things because I was following the Spirit.

When holidays came around, I heard about all the fun and jokes when my family got together. I saw pictures of it online, saw my mom, sisters, and cousins bonding again (with the exception of my dad). It's really family traditions that make a holiday feel like a holiday, and there I was, alone.

Finances were always the biggest and main struggle in my family, and for a long time, visiting home was just not an option. My grandma and my uncle passed away, and I wasn't there to say good-bye to them. My first niece was born, and I couldn't meet her. Rachel and Scott went to the temple, and I wasn't there. I was here, being treated like I was this diseased and contagious monster.

The temptation to quit, to go back to where things were easier and where things made sense, was indescribable at that point.

It never occurred to me that my appearance could cause such a trial in my life. It was so bizarre and new to me, coming from my New York culture, to the point that I was completely unequipped for and lost on how to deal with this new and unwelcome attention. I became mad. I was so hurt. I don't have words adequate enough to describe it properly. How could things be so hard when I was following the Spirit?

Then it just hit me. I didn't want to feel like that anymore. Whatever you're looking for, you'll find it, and I was unconsciously just noticing the bad. It's a toxic way of living. Sometimes we just need to stop, take a break and a deep breath, and refocus on why we're here and what we need to be doing.

I remember having to make a decision. It's a decision I had to make and continue to make; it's a decision *you* have to make every single day: choose to get mad, choose to get bothered or offended, *or* choose to not. Choose to keep going, choose to trust, *choose* to have faith—or not. What it came down to and what it will always come down to is this: choose God or don't. So I had to re-decide who I wanted to follow.

And I decided to keep going. I decided to see what on earth Heavenly Father had up His sleeve for me, because I hadn't the slightest idea. I wasn't going to let anything, no rude comments or dirty looks, get in between me and my eternal salvation. I wasn't going to let anything stop me from the happiness that comes from the gospel. Nothing was going to affect my relationship with my Father in Heaven.

How easy would it have been to yell at that man at Café Rio? How easy would it have been to get mad and him and everyone else, to be offended? It would have been so easy to not just take it out on him or the people of that city but to be upset and mad toward Heavenly Father for leading me here. A place with so many trials and so few answers—answers that would have been comforting during those frequent experiences. How hard it was to have just been baptized, with such small knowledge of the gospel, and be treated that way by fellow brothers and sisters in the gospel.

Yeah, it would have been easy to feel and react that way. But I fought it. I decided otherwise. I turned to this man in Café Rio, introduced myself, and shook his hand. I smiled so big and simply said, "I just got baptized, and this is my first day here!" I said it with happiness, with pride, and with confidence.

How differently things would have gone if I didn't do that.

Faith is not something you just have; it's something you constantly have to work toward. Faith is not a feeling; it's a decision you have to make every day, sometimes several times a day, in each situation. And I already chose who I wanted to follow, didn't I?

That is what happens when you get baptized.

It comes back to that question I had following my baptism and my family's disapproval: "How do you teach someone who doesn't want to listen? How do you teach someone you may never get to speak with or meet?" You teach by example.

We always have to keep in mind that everyone is at different spots in life. Everyone needs to learn different things in different ways. Maybe I could be the one to help them learn. Maybe you could be. Getting mad would just prove their assumptions right, but if I were to simply be *me* proves otherwise. What others learn could rely on how we choose to react. What will you *choose?* Regardless of our circumstances, we get to decide how our day should be today. Decide how to react. Decide to be happy and positive today. Decide to look for the good. Decide to listen and follow God.

When those times arise, when you have to make that same decision I did, think to yourself, "Is this worth giving up my eternal salvation?" Is that comment your ward member said to you worth giving up your eternal happiness? Is that look someone just gave you worth giving up the profound, indescribable blessings Heavenly Father has to give to you? Is it worth stopping yourself from returning to live with Him again? Is it worth your exaltation? "Look to God and live" (Alma 37:47).

Sometimes we can't help but think how much easier it would be if things had gone the way we wanted them to go. But little do we know what's right around the corner for us when we choose to remember God—opportunities that await, the people, the growth, and the blessings. We find whatever it is we're looking for. Look for the good; it's there.

Hard? Yes, undoubtedly. Worth it? Profoundly.

You will not be asked to do something that won't be the absolute best for you. Nothing goes unnoticed. To all those who feel they do not fit in, I tell you with confidence that you're wrong. To all those who are afraid to return because of past mistakes, I say, come! To all those who sit there, offended and holding yourselves back, I ask, is it still worth it?

Don't let anything or anyone stand in the way of following the Spirit, of following Him, of doing what you're supposed to be doing. Nothing is worth giving up your forever happiness.

This gospel *is* for you. These blessings and promises *are* for *you*. You belong as a part of this. This, what we're a part of, is real and so great! This is the greatest thing we could ever be a part of, and I love that. Don't lose sight of why we are here. Don't let others alter the truth of what we should be doing. The truth is that our trials and our circumstances will never alter the unchanging truth that this is all real. This is it. This is what we have, what we were given. This is what we can do. I have to—we have to. We have everything to lose if we don't.

Can you think of anything more important than "endless life and happiness" (Mosiah 16:11)? "Fear not, little flock; . . . let earth and hell combine against you" (D&C 6:34).

God is for us, so it really doesn't matter who is against us.

Part 2

- Your Story -

Chapter 10 . . .

BLOGGING & SPEAKING

> If you are willing and if you just try, you will find yourself in places you never would have dreamed of, doing things you never would have thought of, and becoming better, becoming the person Heavenly Father has wanted you to become all along. AND WHAT A FEELING THAT IS!

GOD AND HIS PROMISES and His help are always there. To see them, all it took was changing my mind-set, that's it. If you look for rude people, for the negative, you will find it. If you look for the positive, you will find it.

Andy and I stayed really close still, and he ended up coming out to Utah later. I was there when he got his mission call to serve in the California San Diego Mission. A big part of me was upset because he got endowed before me; that was something I had been striving toward more vigorously than anything else in my life at that time. But how exciting it was to see him doing so well!

All the emails I received from him were about how awesome things were going and how much he loved his mission. He had been out a month or two when I had received an email from him about a baptism he had coming up that week.

That was the last time I would ever hear from him.

It wasn't until a month after it happened that I found out Andy was home in New York. He left his mission without telling anyone. He didn't tell me. He didn't tell his companion. He didn't tell his mission president. His dad had not only been sending him anti-Mormon articles but also sent him a plane ticket. Andy snuck out in the middle of the night and flew himself home. He blocked everyone online. He left the Church and is now back to the life he lived before he met the elders.

One thing worse than someone not having the gospel is someone having the gospel and not doing anything with it or leaving it. I saw Andy change. I saw him happy. I saw him serve. I saw him affect and help so many people. And just like that, he was facing the other direction.

The missionaries back in New York truly were the greatest examples of the gospel to me in every way. It wasn't because they didn't struggle or were perfect, or even perfectly obedient. I knew very well that they weren't. But when I saw them serving and teaching, I really could see the mantle of the calling upon them and the Lord making their efforts great to help His children. At first, moving to Utah was like being behind the scenes for me. Because I hadn't had the gospel for so long and saw what it did for me, it had never once occurred to me that some people had the gospel and didn't do anything with it. The thought of it devastated me. It had never once occurred to me that some missionaries didn't leave for their missions on time because they lacked desire or didn't even want to serve. It had never crossed my mind that most of the population my age and younger had never even read the Book of Mormon all the way through—or even past 1 Nephi.

Someone in my ward at that time messaged me on Facebook. I didn't know her, but I knew that she went to church every Sunday. She told me of her struggles finding her way back to the gospel. Back? According to her attendance, she never left.

Among those situations and several more, I constantly started thinking, *Heavenly Father, how on earth can I help them?* I just felt so overwhelmed with a desire to help everyone. Member or not, old or young, I couldn't think of anything more important to me than having people who would listen know that they are never alone and they can be happy, that comfort could be felt even in the darkest and most confusing of times. I wanted them to know that help is always available, that they matter, that they make a difference, that they are good enough. They have a God, and He is theirs! He is theirs to keep, to turn to *always*. And there's power in that. He has *all* the power and *wants* to use it personally and individually for you, to give you greater blessings than you even knew existed. All we have to do is turn to Him and try.

Life without God is life without *real* happiness. I know that. I know that because I went twenty-one years of my life thinking that it came from somewhere else, and it doesn't. Even with trials, I wanted to help people cling to the gospel when they felt like their prayers weren't being heard, when they had doubts and questions, or even if they just wanted to know if God truly was there and if He really *did* know them and their struggles and feelings. I wanted them to know that it is possible because I experienced it over and over again. I learned firsthand that we can overcome absolutely everything because of that never-changing, never-weakening, never-wavering love Heavenly Father has for us. He will do anything to get us back.

What could I do? I prayed several times a day, telling God that I wanted nothing more than to help people find their way back to their God. *"Go forth; to them that sit in darkness"* (1 Nephi 21:9).

Because of prayer, I started a blog. I wasn't strong in writing, but I was observant and honest. Everyone has different stories and different experiences, but to think people don't have the same emotions is ludicrous. Everyone's felt alone. Everyone's felt scared. Everyone's felt confused. Weak. Tempted. Mad at God. I wanted them to know my struggles and my lessons because I just wanted people to know they weren't alone in their feelings and that they needed to keep going. They needed to know there is always someone there who not only knows perfectly but also knows how to heal and keep you going. He knows the way because He is the way.

I didn't think anything of my blog. It started out as only a handful of people reading it, and I think they only read it because they felt bad no one else was reading it. But I didn't actually think people would really read it anyway. If I had, I would have named it something better.

When you pray saying you want to help, Heavenly Father will be quick to answer that prayer. But we have to be willing to hear something different than we initially had in mind. Don't shut the door on the Spirit when a different idea comes. Trust it. The Spirit is your friend who works not just with you or by your side but *in* you, and who works directly with Heavenly Father. Because of the Spirit, I then started to make YouTube videos, figuring that there were plenty of people who don't want to read and would much rather listen or watch something instead. My main goal was to just reach as many people as I could. And if you had asked me if making videos was something I did as a hobby, I would tell you that it wasn't. I had no idea how to film or edit or anything. I felt like Nephi when he was asked to build a ship: "Heavenly Father I don't know how to build a . . . you still want me to? I'll just figure it out." And though compared to what so many people are doing it is nothing big, it has been an incredible resource, getting much bigger than I ever anticipated. I started to voice record my blogs and offer them as audio files for listening.

I started to speak. I never sought after speaking. Actually, despite my straight As in college, the one class I failed pretty miserably in was public speaking. But because of that simple prayer of wanting to help and be His hands, I speak in public more frequently than anything else. Heavenly Father was not fooling when He told us He can make our weaknesses become strengths.

Speaking stemmed from bearing my testimony in sacrament; which turned into sharing my thoughts during someone's Young Women lessons; which turned into a young single adult fireside; which turned into a stake fireside; which turned into traveling all over the state of Utah; which has now turned into flying to other states across the nation; which turned into speaking twice with General Young Women President Bonnie Oscarson; which turned into speaking to over 23,000 people with Elder Andersen.

During one year, I spoke as frequently as six times a week, sometimes twice in a day. It was wild and *incredibly* humbling. I never got paid to do any of it, nor did I ever care to. Most times I would spend so much money on gas to travel to speak that I didn't have enough money for groceries or rent. But I couldn't think of anything else I'd rather be doing than serving the Lord. And when you're serving the Lord, of course everything works out, and you will always have the resources you need to continue. I'd work full time, and when the work day ended, I'd hop right in the car—sometimes leaving early or taking unpaid vacation time to take the day off completely—and go speak. I'd spend my nights driving to who-knows-where, praying so hard that my old two-door Alero Oldsmobile wouldn't break down. Sometimes I'd get there early and sit in the parking lot and cry because of how exhausted I was from traveling so long and so frequently. Then I'd spend my nights back in the car, saying that prayer again that it wouldn't break down, and get home late at night, hoping I'd sleep enough to have some energy to do it again the next day.

But I would not trade or change a single thing. I have seen a lot of incredible places, big cities to small towns in the middle of nowhere with not too much to offer anyone. But I found *great* beauty in them (and really good food). I have met a lot of incredible people, mostly people struggling, but I found beauty and strength in them, although they did not feel strong. I was changed and humbled and am better because of them and their efforts.

I don't blog or speak because I am strong; it's actually the opposite. I blog because I am weak, because I rely on Him so deeply. Strong? No. Driven and passionate? Absolutely. I'll be the first to tell you I am far from perfect. In fact, I purposely am really open about my faults and my challenges to everyone, especially in my blogging and speaking. There is so much more that I could be doing and am not. And I could be doing much better at the things I am doing; I know that. Every day I'm reminded of that. But what it is you need to know is that if you are willing and if you just try, you will find yourself in places you never would have dreamed of, doing things you never would have thought of, becoming better, becoming the person Heavenly Father has wanted you to become all along. And what a feeling that is!

Speaking has been one of the greatest and most humbling blessings in my life. The one thing I love more than the gospel is yappin' about it to others. I feel most comfortable, most like myself when I am speaking. I feel alive! I may not have a black name tag, but I believe it is everyone's mission to help people.

My favorite part about speaking is twofold. The first part is sitting on the stand right before I'm about to get up and speak and looking out at everyone. I love it. During the opening hymn, scanning over all those who came, I am able to feel just a sliver of what God feels for them. Just a quick, small glimpse to how He sees them. And just that sliver is overwhelming. It's powerful. It's physical. It's beyond humbling.

My next favorite part is after speaking. Every time I speak, I stay to meet people. I love hearing from them. I love hearing their brief testimonies, their struggles and trials, their losses and gains, their opportunities, blessings, and miracles. I love every bit of it. I love meeting those who feel they are not where they want to and should be. I love meeting those in the middle of a hard time, those who just got through a hard time, those who are doing the right thing on the right path. I love meeting those who are crying, those who cannot bring themselves to say anything to me but just hold my hand and look me in the eye, and I can just *feel.* I love it. I love everyone. To see just how personal and individual Heavenly Father truly is in helping and loving us is the most incredible and indescribable experience. *That* is where I am able to find my strength. That is where my inspiration comes from: *you.*

I never sought after the life I lead now. I never sought after blogging or speaking or being in any "spotlight." But I did seek after service and after helping people know of the joy of the gospel and the love from our God. After living twenty-one years of my life without the gospel, it makes me sick to my stomach to know that there are so many others living without it or not understanding or taking advantage of it. A simple prayer of, "Lord, what can I do to help?" and accepting the Lord's opportunities—no matter how terrifying or bizarre or confusing or hard they may seem when they arrive—has led me to these humbling opportunities in my life that I could not imagine living without.

I wanted to serve a mission. How hard it is to pray, asking for something that means so much to you, and be denied. Especially when it is a righteous, good thing to want to do. It took about two years of being in Utah before I maybe started to get a little glimpse of *why* I needed to move and sacrifice so much and struggle for so long. But looking back, I see that Heavenly Father did give me what I desired so much but in a greater way than I could have known existed as an option for myself. As I am writing this and seeing how much time and energy I spent on trying to figure out the *why* of things, I realize that the *why* in following the Spirit isn't as important as just knowing who is behind it. Fear, confusion, or anger should never be an option for us once we remember who is speaking to and guiding us. He knows you. He knows what you want *and* need. It's just that His ways are greater, and they always will be.

I don't blog so people will know me. I blog so people will want to know God and know with confidence that God knows them. I blog and speak so people will know they are not alone, they are good enough, they can do this, and they are so loved. Everything will be more than just all right. I don't make a single cent from speaking; I do it simply because the gospel is real and it has forever changed me. I am happy because of it, and I want others to feel what I feel. I blog and speak because I truly do care and I promised Him that I'd help.

But it's not about me, nor will it ever be.

It's about you. It's about God. It's about overcoming, becoming better, and being happy. It's about returning. What an extraordinary journey we're on!

An *Ensign* article by Elder Russell M. Nelson called "The Peace and Joy of Knowing the Savior Lives" said something simple that brought a life-changing perspective to me. He was talking about the birth of Christ, the story of Mary:

"Perhaps they traveled even farther. . . . They likely camped out several nights because their journey would have required three to four days" (December 2011).

I don't often think of what they went through as they traveled. I don't often think of the discomfort Mary was in (which, after being pregnant and having a baby myself, I know must have been *pretty* uncomfortable). I don't often think of all the opportunities that came up that didn't work out for her, how badly she wanted a place in the inn but was denied. That seemed like such an amazing thing, and how heartbreaking it was when it didn't work out.

Was it because Mary was being punished? Did she do something wrong? No, not at all.

But Heavenly Father had something else in mind: a manger. It may not have seemed perfect to Mary and Joseph—not what they had in mind at all. But it was all a part of Heavenly Father's plan.

Elder Russell M. Nelson said, "When they reached Bethlehem, the time came for the birth of the Holy Child."

Jesus could have been born any one of those days traveling. But he wasn't born until the time and place were what Heavenly Father needed.

Could you imagine if Mary and Joseph didn't keep going? Or if they were accepted into the inn? Would the shepherds have found them? Would they have been there to bless others and to fulfill the plan and prophecies?

Surely the birth of Christ was perfect in every way. It was the best way rather than a good or a better way because it was *His*. It was according to plan.

So we, too, should wait for our "manger," our best something, rather than settling for something good or something better. Wait for our perfect something, according to Him. I know it can be hard and full of discomfort, just like Mary experienced. But when you see opportunities pass, keep going with faith, knowing there is something else to come. You are not being punished. And when it is His time, it will happen almost immediately. It will not just bless you but profoundly help and bless others because of it, because you waited, because you trust Him, because you know that "*he will not fail thee*" (Deuteronomy 31:8).

Utah may have not been what I had in mind, but it was my "manger."

I used to say that sacrifice is never a bad thing if we have a testimony. But really, something cannot be a sacrifice if we are getting *more* in return. You may not have gone where you had in mind, but you *will* end up where you need to be, with better blessings.

Life is what we do, not what we say we'll do or what we wait around for. God can't help and bless us if we are not moving and if we are not trying. This is a gospel of action, of doing, sharing, growing, and overcoming. It's all about becoming better, more like our Savior. It's about trusting His ways and doing things you never thought you could. As we increase our efforts and just *try,* we will better understand and personally see how loving and powerful Heavenly Father truly is. We will be able to see our potential and be surprised where we end up in life, receiving and enjoying in abundance the greatest things in life. God does care. Do not get discouraged. It will come, and it will be incredible.

Chapter 11 . . .
CHANGE

> Change is always available. Help is always there. Comfort and healing are always there, because CHRIST IS ALWAYS THERE. And He will never look at you like a waste of time.

SEVERAL YEARS AGO I traveled a few hours from where I lived to speak to one of the smallest groups I've spoken to yet. It was a Saturday morning, and all the girls had just woken up and finished eating breakfast around the fire. I was there to end their Young Women retreat, so when I finished, they would pack up and leave to go home. After I spoke, the bishop stood up to give some closing remarks, and he asked us all a question: "What is the most important principle of the gospel?"

"Prayer." "Sacrament." "Reading scriptures." The girls yelled out tons of great answers, ones that would have been my answer had I responded vocally, but he kept shaking his head no.

"The most important principle of this gospel," he said, "is that people can change."

I have been able to speak at Utah State Prison five times now (three on the men's side, twice on the women's), and I have been forever changed by it. I have been to some really incredible and beautiful places and met hundreds of great people a day. I have heard tons of different stories, backgrounds, challenges, and successes. *All* have had some sort of impact on me, and still the prison has been my absolute favorite places I have ever been. I'll share a little bit of what I wrote in my personal journal after my first time speaking to the men's side in March of 2013:

"I can't express what I felt. . . . The Spirit I felt was beyond what I had felt before—it was incredibly powerful. I didn't want to leave and lose how I felt. I was surprised by their example. They all came single-file into the gym, all wearing their matching white inmate uniforms, every single one of them holding a Book of Mormon and a journal on their *own* will. Their humble eyes staring at me was completely captivating. . . . After I spoke, I was able to stay as they separated into groups, and my eyes filled with tears as I heard their goals and desires—their passion to get out just so they can baptize their son or be sealed to their family, to simply sit in a church building. To hear inmate investigators quote D&C more beautifully than I had ever heard before from any member . . . I was truly among incredible, incredible people and was so humbled to meet them. When it was time to leave, a lot of them thanked me and shook my hand. You know how sometimes you can look at someone and you just know they're truly a great person, you can just feel it? I saw that and I felt that with every single eye I looked into. It moved me to literal tears. It moved me to change, to become better, because of their example and greatness that I saw in them."

When I went back to the men's side a year and a half later, it was a little different. It was for a drug addiction program graduation, a challenge I am not familiar with myself. I was told that not only could I not speak on my religion, but I couldn't even mention God at all. What was I supposed to talk about?

I spoke on change.

Although my second time back to the prison was not a religious service in any degree, and most definitely not an LDS service, a one-time choir of inmates got up to sing just for this occasion. I was completely shocked at their choice of song: "A Child's Prayer." The most intimidating men you could imagine—these big, tall, buff men, all ages from twenties up to some in maybe their late seventies, some missing most of their teeth, most with tattoos on their face and head—started singing, "Heavenly Father, are you really there?"

I sat on their makeshift stage, and I lost it. The Spirit overwhelmed me so physically—more than I have ever felt before in my entire life. Because God was there. Because regardless of where they were and what they had done, He was aware of them. They were not alone. And I felt so powerfully that they never had been.

Neither are you.

I hate the phrase, "That's just who I am." When you think that, you deny the power of Christ. The power of change is very real, and although there are many people who do not make the decision to change for the better, we all have that power to change. People change every day. I am not who I was six years ago. The group I spoke to at the prison—they are not who they used to be. They were full of greatness; I could feel it. I am changed and better because of it.

The road to becoming better seems to get longer and longer with more rocks and bumps and holes and detours than we could have ever imagined. But what seem to be roadblocks and detours along the way are actually paths we don't recognize that lead us to places we never would have thought of and gets us doing things we never would have dreamed of. All of which are better than what we initially had in mind. And through those paths I have taken to be better and become more, I truly feel like I've found me—who I was meant to be all along.

I was thinking for several weeks on the question "What makes people want to change?" I asked many people, and they all told me amazing stories about how they came to realize they needed to be doing something different. They all gave me different responses to that question. After praying about this question many times, I realized that there is only one answer: the Church is true. This is all real, and Heavenly Father loves us and misses us when we are not there. It is the Spirit that makes us want to change, and it is the Savior who makes it possible. "All ye that kindle fire, that compass yourselves about with sparks, walk in the light of your fire and in the sparks which ye have kindled" (2 Nephi 7:11).

Before we came to this earth, there was a big war in heaven, when Satan was cast out and a third of the spirits in the premortal life followed him. Absolutely every single one of us who has ever lived and ever will live, whether we believe in Christ or not, fought on Christ's side. That means *you* fought for Christ. And if you aren't still on His side, now is the best time to come back to His side. When you decide that, you will have already started to become better.

Asking people to be part of this gospel and continue living it is the most personal question we can ask; it's an invitation to change everything about their lives. Yeah, change is hard, and the thought of everything you need to be doing better or stop doing altogether is exhausting in itself sometimes. But it will *always* be possible for every one of us because of Christ. Change is more difficult when we aren't fully committed or don't fully know why we should. Love for and an understanding of Christ can fix that.

Our lack of efforts or knowledge should never lead to anger or doubts toward God's existence. Don't stop living the gospel to find out if it's completely true—live it more fully to more fully know. The more you learn about the gospel, try in church, and make your testimony and relationship with your Father in Heaven stronger, then the more your *desire* to change will increase, and it will become easier to do so. Not easy, but easier.

Before I had the gospel, I had tons of bad habits that I tried several times to quit but couldn't. No matter how promising it started out, I always failed. But when I was changing because of my knowledge of the gospel and love for Christ, it was different. I *wanted* to change and had heavenly reasons, so I had heavenly help to do so. It would have been close to impossible if I wasn't praying for help several times a day throughout the day, every day.

I can count on one hand the number of times Heavenly Father actually speaks in the scriptures. It is usually His Son, Jesus Christ, or the Spirit who speaks. But every one of us can speak to God directly. How cool and sacred is that? When I pray, it helps me to ask Him to help me with my prayer: "Heavenly Father, please help me with this prayer." I've found myself asking for things I never thought of and saying things that haven't come to mind before. Sometimes if I am having a hard time with my prayers, I'll close my eyes and picture my Father in Heaven standing right in front of me. When I do, it becomes a meaningful conversation; I open up more. When we listen during and after our prayers, then answers, understanding, comfort, and strength come.

Distractions stop us from receiving and hearing answers. Inspiration, clarity, and answers come quicker and more frequently when we are regularly reading the scriptures, even if they don't make sense to us at first. It's up to us to seek them out and listen, not just sit idly waiting for them to show up in our laps. Spiritual idleness is spiritual suicide.

Our God is an unchanging God. His commandments don't change, and neither does His love, personally and individually, for you, regardless of where you are in life.

To those who have uncertainties, questions, or doubts, I say, get started, keep going, and keep trying. To those struggling to overcome or change, I say, keep going, keep trying, and keep praying. Communication with your God, your Father in Heaven, is essential. God wants to hear from you, so talk to Him! You are *always* worthy to pray and to turn to Him. You will never be "too far gone" to turn to Him or for Him to help you, heal you, and forgive you. You are always worthy of your God's help and attention because of that unchanging love He has for you—unwavering, never-weakening, ever-present, just for you, personally and individually. "A shepherd hath called after you and is still calling after you" (Alma 5:37).

There are no words that can properly express how precious and sacred the change is that takes place in someone when they allow themselves to partake of the restored gospel by their efforts to live the commandments.

It's in the trying that our efforts are blessed, even if we slip up. He smiles at our efforts, even if we aren't there yet. I heard a metaphor several years ago about a man on the side of the road with a broken car. One man says a prayer and waits for something or someone to come and fix it. The other man also says a prayer and then works to try to get it running again. Which man will have a fixed car sooner? The one acting. "Take responsibility and go to work so that there is something for God to help us with" (D. Todd Christofferson, "Free Forever, to Act for Themselves," *Ensign*, November 2014). "And I said: Lord, how is it done? And he said unto me: Because of thy faith in Christ" (Enos 1:7–8).

Satan will not give up, and it's through the smaller things that he slowly gets us. We have to continuously be conscious of what we're doing and striving toward. The gospel is like running up the downward escalator: the moment you pause, you start sliding back. Satan waits for the moment you slow down to try and get you.

I have come to notice that Satan gets to us in our thoughts more than he does with our actions. He tells us that we aren't good enough, that we never will be, and that we aren't worthy to pray or be forgiven. Do not listen to those thoughts. If you think Heavenly Father will do anything to stop you from overcoming and conquering, you're wrong. Blessings and help will always be there for you, even if you feel like you don't deserve them. He wants us to succeed. He wants us back home and misses us even when we are a little distant from Him. Everyone can be forgiven when we turn to Him and repent. "As oft as they repented and sought forgiveness, with real intent, they were forgiven" (Moroni 6:8).

Take confidence in the blessings He has given us. When you repent—no matter who you are or where you came from—when you move away from sin and move forward to God, you are always forgiven, and your sins are always forgotten. To Him, they are gone. To us, they become testimony. Knowledge. Strength.

I received a priesthood blessing once that said, "You are clean in front of God. When He sees you, He does not see your past or what's on your body. And He personally weeps with you when you don't see that in yourself."

The more I read my email from people sharing their stories, the more I see that many of us want to come back and make those steps but are afraid of what others may think. They're afraid of being judged. It makes me think of many experiences, but I'll go back to the story I mentioned previously in Café Rio and about my tattoos.

I met with the mission president before baptism. As I was walking in to the most nerve-racking meeting of my entire life, my elders decided then was the best time to tell me, "Oh, by the way, the prophet says you're not allowed to get any more tattoos. Okay, go get 'em!"

Tattoos really were just part of my culture, not rebellion. It's hard to spot someone without a tattoo where I'm from. When I got baptized, I thought I'd always like them and have the desire to get more but that I wouldn't act on it because my desire to follow the prophet was stronger. That wasn't the case; the desire was gone. As I learned, tried, and participated in the gospel, my desires completely changed on their own. My interest in tattoos completely disappeared.

"But this one thing I do, forgetting those things which are behind, and reaching forth unto those things which are before" (Philippians 3:13).

I never thought much about tattoos or even the fact that I had them until I moved to Utah. The first time they became an issue was when I felt judged, confused, and ignored, when others looked at me in disgust and moms pulled their children away from me. I was judged for who I used to be, not who I was and who I was becoming. I was treated so poorly for how I looked, not specifically because of the tattoos but because they showed outwardly that at one point I didn't live the way they were taught we should live. They never realized that I didn't grow up a member.

It was heartbreaking to be treated so poorly, to be judged for being someone I wasn't anymore. People looked at me like I was the modern-day Korihor. It was so hard that on my weak days I would stay home because I couldn't handle the stares and rude comments. But that was before the change of mind-set came and turned it all around.

But whether you did something you knew was wrong or, like me, didn't realize what you were doing was wrong, it is irrelevant. It wouldn't have mattered whether I got those tattoos before I was baptized or grew up in the Church and got them. And why is that?

Because of Christ. Whatever you have done—whether you knew it was wrong or not, whether physically visible or not—you can move past it. Everyone can be forgiven. You can always be forgiven, because of Christ.

I am assuming most of you reading this do not have tattoos of your own, but what about your "tattoos"—your past mistakes, habits, or wrongdoings? How do you move past those, especially when you think people know them or judge you by them? God does not see yours either. Not when we change. Not when we try. Not when we turn to Him.

And how am I able to do everything I am doing now? How was I able to serve in the temple and in different presidencies? Because God does not see me as "The Tattooed Mormon." Because God does not see any of my tattoos; to Him, they are completely gone.

And for you? God does not see your "tattoos," not when you change and try—not when you turn to Him and use this faith you may think you don't have at times.

"He who has repented of his sins, the same is forgiven, and I, the Lord, remember them no more" (D&C 58:42).

I absolutely hate the nickname "The Tattooed Mormon." I never call myself that and prefer that others not refer to me as that either. I think talking about what is on my skin is completely irrelevant to where I am now in life and what I want the focus of my efforts to be on. I got the nickname from a blog post I named in conscious efforts to avoid even bringing up tattoos in the post at all, because I really didn't want that to be the point. I figured having it subtly in the title I could avoid missing the point of the actual post about the incredible power of the Atonement. I never imagined it would be an awful label that I can't seem to shake no matter how hard I point others away from myself and toward Christ.

Calling me the tattooed Mormon is hardly any different than calling someone the "used-to-smoke Mormon" or the "used-to-look-at-pornography Mormon." I'm not saying tattoos are next to those sins, but I am saying that it is calling someone by who they no longer are—by what they are no longer doing and a part of. And why would anyone ever want to do that? We most definitely would not like it if others did that to us. Because of repentance, because of Christ and His Atonement, my tattoos are not something God chooses to overlook, but they *in reality* do not exist at all. *That* is what the Atonement does. Maybe one day I won't be known as the tattooed Mormon to the world, but maybe just the happy Mormon or hopefully just the Mormon who is simply trying to help others. Just like the title of this book says, I am so much more than that.

And you—there is so much greatness in you, and you are so *much more* than the mistakes you've made.

Do not let who you used to be hold you back from who you can become. Holding yourself back is frustrating everything the Atonement stands for and is. "How could ye have rejected that Jesus, who stood with open arms to receive you!" (Mormon 6:17).

The Atonement is there for every single one of us. How do we use it in our lives? By turning to Him, talking to Him, and *trusting* Him. In 3 Nephi 17, Christ asked for all those that were "afflicted in *any* manner" (verse 7; emphasis added) to go to Him so that He would heal them. And "he did heal them every one as they were brought forth unto him" (verse 9). Help and healing are there, but just like in that scripture, we can't receive it if we do not go to Him.

Do not hold yourself back. Do not shortchange yourself. It is not Christ who is not there for us; we are not there for Him, to *let* Him help and change and heal us. If we feel that Heavenly Father has turned His back on us, we're the ones who need to turn around.

"Will ye not now return unto me, and repent of your sins, and be converted, that I may heal you?" (3 Nephi 9:13).

An older woman in one of my wards once said, "If we've never been offended by someone at church, then we don't go often enough." When those times arise that someone may offend you, just remember: "Is this worth giving up my eternal salvation?"

If you feel like you don't fit in or if you are afraid to return, remember, this gospel is for you. These blessings and promises are for you because you belong as a part of this. No sacrifice isn't worth the blessings we will be getting in return. You can do it, and your Lord will not let you do it on our own. If all you know is that you need to change but aren't sure what or how, know that you can ask Him. Ask Him who He wants you to be and to show you what to do next and how to do it. Just get started. Make efforts every day. Set goals. Say prayers. Work hard. God will never look at you like you're a waste of time.

Never let fear decide your future. Fear is one of the adversary's finest tools. Whether you have to change your whole life around or change just a few small things, whether you have to lose friends and do it on your own or have the support of those around you, whether you have to experiment or just follow through with the things you already know, whether it is hard or easy—you will be happy and it will be great. It will be the greatest thing you do, and you will be the happiest you have ever been. No matter how far you are from where you should be, those steps you take closer to that point will be the most important and the most rewarding.

I have learned and relearned that sometimes God asks us to do hard things. Sometimes He asks us to leave our family and move across the country. Sometimes He asks us to lose all our friends and be persecuted. Sometimes He doesn't give us all the answers and allows us to walk blindfolded, holding His hand. But the blessings He gives us in return are always greater than what we knew was even available for us.

If you want a new tomorrow, then make new choices today. Don't wish for it; work for it. What is coming is better than what is gone. Now is not the time for God to judge us but to love and help us. Take advantage of that; don't take it for granted. Be honest and use the Atonement. No matter how painful it is, no matter how "bad" you think you are, no matter how many bad habits you think you have, do not ever stop. You are not alone. Help is there because Christ is there, next to you. And He doesn't just stand there with you; He feels with you. Turn to Him for help and forgiveness, and when you receive it, make sure you forgive yourself as quickly as God forgives you. Forgive yourself and move on. God has.

It's not what we do once in a while that shapes our lives but what we do consistently. Every day try a little harder, and don't slow down. Be better than who you were yesterday. When we become comfortable, we stop growing. Always exercise your change-of-heart muscle. Keep going and keep growing. Don't you stop. Do not get discouraged.

Every day—every passing second—is a chance to turn it all around. Strive every day to be a little better, to be the best you. Believe in yourself and believe in God. You are always worthy of your God's love and help.

Refocus on what matters most in life. Be patient with yourself, and most important, be proud of yourself, of the steps—no matter how small they seem to you—that you have taken to become better. Be proud that you are trying, even if you aren't there yet. Be proud and throw out any sliver of discouragement with your efforts, because it is when we try and act that we are blessed. We are blessed for our efforts of *trying*, not perfection. Change is always available. Help is always there. Comfort and healing are always there because Christ and *your* Father in Heaven are always available to you. Always.

Today is the start of anything you want. Life is short; don't be lazy. I promise that you can live the commandments and still be cool. It happens all the time—it's like a thing. How grateful I am for commandments and for covenants. I am here, and I am happy because of them. I am nothing without them. Covenants and commandments should never be approached as a burden or approached apprehensively, but rather they should be sought after and embraced with joy and excitement to be able to partake more fully of the best *ever* created.

Today, comfort, answers, strength, happiness, a chance to change, and a chance to become better are available. So smile! And smile tomorrow too. Because today, tomorrow, and every day after that, we have all that we need available to us because of Christ.

Chapter 12 . . .

TRIALS

> Never let a trial or a change of course take away from the unchangeable truth that GOD IS TAKING CARE OF YOU.

TOWARD THE END OF 2013, John Bytheway and I flew together to Temecula, CA, and both spoke at a mid-single's conference. He told me a story that I will never forget, and by "never forget" I mean, I mostly forgot the story but not the message.

He told me of when he was younger and was having a particularly hard time, and he spoke with his bishop, who told him, "Don't worry, John. This will pass." And he was right! The next day John felt much better and was filled with comfort and understanding and happiness! He happened to see his bishop that day and said, "Bishop, you're right! It did pass!" His bishop responded, "John, *this too* shall pass."

And so it is with life! It's filled with really incredible days when you achieve and give and receive much. You feel unstoppable, productive, strong, and happy. You feel particularly close to the Lord and His Spirit.

And then there are those difficult days—weak days, sick days, lonely days, and stressful days—that leave you drained. Days where guidance and the Spirit are hard to feel, and it's hard to find energy or faith to even seek them out. Days where you wonder where God is and question His hand in your life.

Life is hard. And things have proven to only get more difficult as time goes on. I've had to pass through trials more difficult than losing my friends, picking between the gospel and my dad, being locked in an office and screamed at for being a member, being denied serving a mission, or moving across the country by myself to be treated so poorly when I arrived. Those were not the last times I yelled at God or felt alone. Those trials were not the peak of my hardest times. I have been asked by God to pass through even harder trials than those.

It's in the unexpected and unwanted difficult times that we have those fleeting thoughts: "Are you even there still? Do you even care about *me?* Do you even exist?"

I was just reading through my journal and came across this entry I wrote: "I'm not this strong. I can't do this. I feel awful. I feel like I literally have nothing. I feel empty. I feel abandoned. This is too much. Why won't God remove this already? Hasn't it been long enough? How long do I have to endure? I am heavy with burden. So heavy that I cannot move. I feel broken. I am heavy. I am literally and physically completely weighted down with burden. My soul and my heart ache. My energy and my strength have run thin."

Humility has been a constant companion in my trials, as I'm sure it has been for you as well. It's incredible to see how teachable we are with the humility that comes from those difficult, hard, trying times we go through. When your strength has run thin, when you feel your prayers are unanswered, when you feel you have been left alone—those are the most precious times to be had. Those times are the gems in life. When you feel at your weakest, you are in fact your strongest. When we are convinced, even just for a moment, that Heavenly Father has left us crying out what Joseph Smith and Christ themselves felt to cry out—"O God, where art thou?" (D&C 121:1; see also Matthew 27:46; Mark 15:34)—those are the exact moments He is the closest to us. They are, I assure you.

I know how hard things can be. I know how hard it is to keep going sometimes—how tiring and discouraging and lonely. But I also know how worth it and possible it is to keep going, to push forward, to conquer, and to be *happy* if we just turn to Him.

Force yourself to say a prayer no matter how frustrated you are. Pray hardest when it's hardest to pray. It was in those honest prayers (with me yelling at Him) that I received more detailed comfort and counsel. It's important to vent and open up fully and completely to your Father in Heaven. But it is crucial to listen—and not just listen to what we want to hear. As Elder Richard G. Scott says, "Sometimes answers to prayer are not recognized because we are too intent on wanting confirmation of our own desires" ("Learning to Recognize Answers to Prayer," *Ensign*, November 1989).

Life is not about picking what we want to do and just asking for Heavenly Father's help with it; it is about doing what He asks of us and receiving those blessings and help and comfort to follow through.

We often view Laman and Lemuel just as Nephi's wicked brothers but fail to see how similar we are to them. They were visited by an angel of the Lord and had received counsel. Not once did they deny the fact that they saw an angel, but they "murmured" because they felt that what they believed and what they had in mind was right or better.

Laman, Lemuel, and Nephi are perfect examples of continuing forward. They were commanded by God to go and obtain the records from Laban, and they failed. They failed more than once. How easy it would have been to be mad at God or confused and discouraged. If God commanded it, why didn't it work out? But it wasn't until they abandoned their ideas and listened to God's that they accomplished it—or Nephi accomplished it. After two failed attempts, Nephi was the only one who inquired of the Lord, and because he did, he was able to succeed. And because Laman and Lemuel did not seek the Lord, they remained where they were, murmuring, with no success.

How many times have we heard God or the Spirit speaking to us but refused to hearken because we were stuck on a certain way we desired for ourselves? I can think of too many times I was upset the Spirit wasn't speaking in a situation where I was asking for answers and counsel. But the reality is the Spirit is always there, but I couldn't hear Him until I realized that my desires or ideas may not be right or best.

Nephi's success came when he went forward with faith that the Lord would provide a way, when he was open and willing to accept God's way and not his own. Though I personally think Laman and Lemuel's ways were more logical to me than Nephi killing Laban with a sword, I don't know if success would have come if Nephi allowed logic (or worldly thinking) to overrule the Spirit.

During trials it's easy to allow passing time to dim the promises we've received from our Father in Heaven. Blessings and promises given to us never expire. We must never lose sight of who is helping and guiding us and embrace the unexpected and unplanned. Never let a change of course take away from the unchangeable truth that God is taking care of you. You will never be asked to do anything that would not be for the absolute best for you. "Know ye not that ye are in the hands of God? Know ye not that he hath all power?" (Mormon 5:23).

Do not allow passing time to weaken your faith in His promises and blessings to you. All of the promises, all of the blessings we are trying so hard to attain are all written in the scriptures as past tense, "prepared." They're already there. Heavenly Father has already spent the time, the love, the work, and the effort in preparing the absolute best ever created. And we can have it. Not just in the eternities, but here, daily, in mortality, if we just keep going and if we just trust Him.

"Come, ye blessed of my Father, inherit the kingdom prepared for you from the foundation of the world" (Matthew 25:34).

Back when I met the elders, they told me, casually I'm sure, to keep a journal. For some reason, I took that seriously and did. It was really what started my writing as a whole. I started a main gospel journal, writing anything that happened to me relating to God and His gospel in *any* way and in *any* degree. Then I started a testimony journal, a journal I write in once a month every fast and testimony day. I write down just how my testimony has strengthened the past month, because if it hasn't, I'm doing something wrong. The best way to strengthen your testimony is to share it, even if it's to yourself. Then I started a journal for notes from general conference. Then I started a baptism journal, which I write in every August 22—where I am in life, what I'm doing, a picture, and my testimony. And I have a priesthood blessing journal—my favorite journal.

When I receive a priesthood blessing, I sit with a notepad and pen in my lap. When "Amen" is said, I'll sit there and write down everything I remember. I started this back in 2010 and now have many years of counsel and blessings worded directly from my Father in Heaven for me specifically. This has proven to be one of my biggest treasures in my trials. How easy it is to let our clouds of trials block our sun. How easy it is to lose sight of what we need to be doing and what is waiting for us to receive. Oftentimes when things are really hard, I'll lie on the floor, pull out this journal, and just read it to move the clouds that block the sun.

There will be many of you reading this right now who are in need of a priesthood blessing. Please, get one. Do not talk yourself out of it. A rule of thumb for me is that if someone asks me if I need one or if the idea comes to my mind, I take that as a nudge from the Spirit and follow through. Because of that, I have had several blessings that started out with, "Heavenly Father wanted to speak to you . . ." How sad it would have been if I missed out on hearing personalized counsel because I actively chose to shrug off the idea. Your situation is never too small or insignificant for a blessing. Nothing is insignificant to your God. Trust me, I know it is not easy for everyone to get one. Living across the country with no family and as a convert, I had to put forth a lot of effort to get a blessing. I never had the luxury of living with a priesthood holder. It took a lot of calls to make it happen, but remember that Heavenly Father *wants* to speak to you; He loves you, and He will help make this possible if you reach out.

Why do bad things happen on days I tried the hardest? This is a question I not only hear from others but also sometimes ask myself. Sometimes, even when our efforts are on point, we still seem to be in the hands of the adversary and can't help but wonder why that is. We are not immune to hard times. Instead of doubting God or the Spirit or doubting your efforts, think of how you were guided that day to do a little extra. Think of how much more difficult it would have been had you *not* tried a little harder that day. The gospel is not there to prevent hard times from coming but to help strengthen and guide us when they do come.

When I first joined the Church and trials started to rain down, all I had was a promise from my missionaries and the Church pamphlets. The only way I knew of to build up true happiness was in these Church pamphlets and the Book of Mormon. Most times I felt like all I had was just Heavenly Father, but in every circumstance, He is just that—all you really need. How great that I had that relationship, just between the Lord and me. This way I was able to leave the worldly things out of it and learn firsthand what the Lord can truly do for me.

You will always have what you need to make it through anything. Comfort is always there because Christ is always there. He knows the way because He is the way. When dark times come, calm your thoughts and listen for Him. "Behold our God is with us, and he will not suffer that we should fall; then let us go forth" (Alma 56:46).

Sometimes answers won't always be there, but strength and comfort always will. Like with my move to Utah, especially when it was so hard, no matter how many times I pleaded to know why, it didn't become clear until years later. In those unclear times, remember the promise He has given to us: "Be of good cheer, for I will lead you along. The kingdom is yours and the blessings thereof are yours, and the riches of eternity are yours" (D&C 78:18).

Yes, life is what we make of it. Or it could be what we *allow* God to make of it for us. Choose God, because once you choose God, anything is possible.

Life has never gone the way I had in mind, not even once. And that can be hard. But I hate to think of my life as any different than it is now. I hate to think what my life would be like had I chosen not to keep going, not to trust, especially in those dark, hard, and confusing times. I wouldn't have a single thing I have now if it weren't for God and His ways.

There will always be something to overcome, something hard to handle, or something new to figure out. How unproductive it is to long for the trial to be over, to crave a fast-forward button, to hang onto that make-believe mortal vision we create in our minds. Stop living in the future, and enjoy today. Search, learn, and find joy in your trials, because surely there will be many, consistent through our whole existence here.

During hard times, it has helped me to ask, "What can I learn from this?" Having that mindset will chase away anger or bitterness and turn your trying times into productive learning times. When Satan gets me down, it's only because I allow him to. In those hard and trying times, look for the calming happiness of the Spirit. It's always there; you have to *allow* yourself to let the Spirit give you peace that this trial is according to plan and it will be better than just okay. It will be incredible and indescribable. You will feel it, and it will strengthen you. Every time. Always.

You have a God, and He is yours. You have a powerful, almighty God whose whole purpose is to help you, love you, and give you the greatest ever created. A God whose every intention is for you to return to Him triumphantly. A God who has already spent time, love, thought, and work into the best ever created for *you*. It is already prepared. He is waiting to give it to us if we just turn to Him and continue.

When hard times come, do not justify the adversary's presence. Allow yourself to feel the happiness that is always there. Forget not that you are not meant to just get by; you're meant to be happy and to triumph gloriously. Forget not that His ways are always better; and how comforting it is to know that He knows us better than we know ourselves, so He can help us in the most perfect way to guide us to things we may not have known we needed. Never should it be about what you don't have or haven't gotten yet. Don't let it be about what you don't know or can't do. Embrace what comes your way, especially that which you didn't initially envision for yourself. Trust Him and allow Him to show you how great your God is.

Do not be ashamed or embarrassed. And more than anything, do not think you cannot do this. Do not let giving up be an option. Focus on Him, knowing that you will be blessed with things greater than you thought available for yourself. What you know and what you have will always be enough for His help and guidance. His hand is always there, never leaving. Prioritize. Turn to Him. Experiment, act, focus, commit, try, hold on, embrace, and receive.

"Have we not reason to rejoice? Yea, I say unto you, there never were men that had so great reason to rejoice as we, since the world began; yea, and my joy is carried away, even unto boasting in my God; for he has all power, all wisdom, and all understanding; he comprehendeth all things" (Alma 26:35).

There are many times in life that could leave you crying on the floor and sometimes yelling at God, but it's then we need to take a step back, take a deep breath, relax, and *listen.* Focus on what's most important: God. And with Him we overcome, conquer, and receive the best ever created. Maybe that's what I love most about the gospel, not that it prevents us from the blows of life but that we can feel an incredible peace and love in every dark moment. Forget not whose hands you're in.

Hard things will not just go away, obviously, but sometimes they may not seem to get better either. Sometimes, *most times,* they will last longer than you may feel you have the faith to last. It wasn't until I was in the middle of one particularly hard trial, when I was lying on the floor, physically exhausted from my burdens, that I reflected on everything I'd been going through and feeling and realized something:

Relief doesn't have to be postponed until a trial is over; it can come with a change of mind-set, a mind-set of hope, seeking, and noticing the small but significant blessings from God that witness He's there. A mind-set and realization that you're still here, you're still standing, and you are not broken. A mind-set that allows yourself to have open eyes to see past our narrow and mortal desires. Even our loneliest and hardest days are, in fact, rich with direction and guidance to move you forward, not backward, on the path God has for you to the best and most fulfilling journey.

"Tell them to fear not, for God will deliver them" (Alma 61:21).

I have a confession . . .

I am weak. I am far from strong. I struggle. But I am oh so happy—full of *real* happiness.

Life is perfect—perfect to learn and grow from. I see old pictures of myself and think of how I had no idea how my life would unfold, no idea what lay ahead or where God would bring me. And to see what I have now and what I'm doing, I can't help but smile. Sometimes as I look back on old pictures or read old journal entries about my trials and confusion, I wish I could just yell to my younger self, "You'll be all right! Your life turns out awesome!" But of course it turns out awesome, because that's what God will always do for us. We may not have all the answers we want about our future, but we know enough: we are led by an all-powerful, all-loving God.

Love where you are—a perfect reminder for when things are hard. Don't spend your time looking ahead, pleading for things to be over and things to be different. Just *stop.* Stop looking backward. Stop yearning for the future. Today, where you are right now, is a joy. Today, right now, is the best place to be. Happiness does await us in this day. His blessings and promises are here, right now. He will not withhold His love and blessings from us just because we are at a different phase of our life. They are not withheld from us if sometimes we are not as strong or as good as we could be. No matter what we have or don't have—no matter what we can or can't do—good times or bad, joy comes now. Happiness is in *today.* God is always mindful of us, there for us, waiting for us, loving us. Even in hard times, life is oh so good. "His hand is stretched out, and who shall turn it back?" (2 Nephi 24:27).

Every trial, hardship, discouragement, and heartache will not be wasted or go unnoticed. Be patient, take a deep breath, and smile. Everything will be all right; we are in the best hands. Push forward with a brightness of hope, and do not let giving up be an option. Stay close to the Lord, even if everything doesn't make sense at first. We will *never* be shortchanged if we are simply trying, even if we feel like our energy and faith have run thin. We have everything we need in the bullet points of the gospel. The power behind every resource we are given to return home is indescribably real and absolutely incredible. "Perish or conquer" (Alma 44:8), you decide.

All things denote there is a God, even your trials. Your prayers have been heard. But greater are the things He has in store for you. Do not get discouraged or lose confidence or faith. Don't do it! Do not stop. Do not forget whose hands you are in. Never are we alone. Heavenly Father is constantly there, guiding, leading, teaching, and helping us. Hold to hope. Always look to God. And allow yourself to seek and listen for the strength and progression that is surely there, day by day, particularly in those hard times.

Forget not perhaps one of the most important blessings He has given us: enjoyment! God wants us to be happy. Take joy in those times. Take joy in your journey, take joy in being taught, in growth, in all of your experiences. Take joy in knowing that you have a God, and He is yours to keep! He is yours to use and turn to, always! He wants to help you, to guide and direct and bless you abundantly with the best that there is. This is a gospel, a journey, a *reality* of happiness! We just need to turn to Him, remembering that He has the best things in store for us, better than we could have ever thought of ourselves.

Arise! Fear not. Take joy in your journey! Receive all that is already created for you, personally and individually. This is so real, and it is so great! Wherefore, continue. Continue always in Him. "I will be with thee: I will not fail thee, nor forsake thee. . . . Be strong" (Joshua 1:5–6).

Chapter 13 . . .
TEMPLE

MAKING AND KEEPING COVENANTS opens the gate to an outpouring of blessings.

EVER SINCE I WAS baptized, my top goal was to go to the temple. I'm not even sure that I fully knew what the temple was when my desire first started, and it quickly grew into an unbearable wait. Within a month of my baptism, I received my limited-use recommend for going with my ward to do baptisms. We would all go once a month and caravan down to the Palmyra Temple.

When I first walked in, I saw this beautiful desk and a line of temple workers from the front door to the stained glass doors that led to the baptistry. All in white gowns. All smiling. Each one of them individually greeted us by shaking our hands as we came in. I felt like I was checking in to heaven.

The temple president would always come and speak to us each time we went as a ward. I'll never forget what he said my first time there and the impression it left on me: "You are walking where the Lord has walked. This is His house, and you are His honored guest."

Being able to listen to the baptism ordinance again was great because I didn't remember it from when I was baptized. Doing ordinances in the name of Christ, it is as if He were doing them Himself. How powerful and cool is that?

But I wanted something more. I didn't want to keep turning to the right into the stained glass doors. I wanted to go straight past the pretty desk. I was thirsty for all the ordinances because I wanted to be as close to the Lord as I could. I was just chasing happiness, and I knew that one of the best ways was just past that desk.

Shortly after baptism, I played a ball game at the church with the missionaries. During the game, I noticed everyone wearing these white undershorts, even the sisters. I had no idea what they were at the time or that they were tied to the temple. No one ever mentioned them to me, yet for some reason, when I saw them I immediately wanted them. For some reason, when I saw them I thought *protection.* When I found out they came from the temple, my urgency to be endowed was through the roof. I wanted my endowment so badly, and I wanted to wear garments so badly. I wanted *everything* from the Lord.

If I'd had it my way, I would have been endowed a month after I was baptized. I thought about the temple literally every day, and it was my top priority. I had a countdown to my anniversary of being a member one year so that I could reach that goal, and in the meantime, I read every book in print about the temple that I could find. I wanted to learn and prepare as much as I could. Just after my one-year anniversary, I went to talk to my bishop to see if I could go through the temple. His answer devastated me.

"Al, I know you are ready, and there isn't anything you can be doing that you aren't already doing, but it's just not time yet."

Stab to the heart. I hated that I was ready and it just wasn't time yet.

It was so hard for me not to become bitter, to see others who were endowed and not be able to go to the temple. Every time I saw someone who was able to go but actively chose not to, I felt like my heart was being squeezed in a vice. Sometimes I'd look at people walking past the front desk and have to hold back tears because that wasn't me. That's how badly I wanted it.

I visited my bishop every month, asking if the Lord had changed His mind yet and if it was time to go. But it wasn't. It wouldn't be time for what seemed to be forever. I made a pact that I was going to go to the temple as often as I could to show the Lord I was committed. I went every Friday, sometimes more often. I thought if I could prove to Heavenly Father I was taking advantage of the ordinances I *could* do, I would be able to speed up His timetable.

Time seems to slow down when you are waiting for something you want. The moment I was waiting for didn't come until a month after the three-year anniversary of my baptism, when I was barely twenty-four years old. Those were three very long years. I still greatly desired to receive my endowment, but it wasn't until one day a few years later when I was waiting to do baptisms, I felt that I didn't belong there and it was finally time. It wasn't that I didn't belong in the temple but that I didn't belong in that section anymore. I went to speak to my bishop about it, and a week and a half later I went to the Provo Temple and received my endowment.

I wasn't going to the temple because I was going on a mission or getting married (which are both awesome and important reasons, as long as you're going for you and for the right reasons). I went because it was really important to me and I wanted to be closer to my Father in Heaven.

I didn't invite anyone to come. And my escort was a woman named Suzanne whom I had only met that week and who was probably shocked that I even asked. I'm not saying that is the best way to do it (in fact, I don't know of anyone else who did it that way, asking a stranger to be your escort), but it was intimate and perfect for me.

When I was finally able to put my garments on, I was so excited that I flung open my dressing room door and in only my garments, in front of three eightyish-year-old temple workers, started to do a dance. I am not kidding. That's how exited I was. Could you imagine the temple workers' faces when I did that? And for anyone who has wondered about garments, they aren't ugly, weird, or uncomfortable, and the promises tied to them are my favorite promises from the temple (if I am allowed to pick favorites). The only negative associations with garments (and I mean this in the nicest, most inoffensive way possible) are tied to prideful and selfish reasons. Here's the deal: temple garments are the only tangible thing you can take with you from the temple, and I feel truly spoiled that I can always have them with me.

Here's a blurb from my testimony journal:

"I left a changed person. Every aspect of my life is better. I even look better. I am better than I was even just a few days ago, and I know I will continue to be better just by going back. That's what the temple does for you. You leave better. You leave stronger. Comforted. Calm. Priorities straightened. Motivated. But it's a physical change, not just spiritually or mentally. And it's not just the first time you go but every time. There is a noticeable contrast. I am a different person. There is a huge contrast. I am protected. My whole life has changed for forever, for the better. I feel it. Jesus Christ lives and works in His home—our temples. And you can feel it. You can take it with you and have it as a part of you. And we can conquer. Triumphantly. We cannot be led in the wrong direction if we are going to the temple. We cannot fail. We can't. I know that if the temple is not the centerpiece of my life, I will not be able to handle the trials that are to come. He has given us literally everything we need. I will return often; that is where I belong."

I'm not exaggerating when I say that during the first months after I went through the temple the first time, I went at least three times a week. I couldn't get enough. The temple was home. I was there so much that, not counting the time I was asleep, I was at the temple more than I was at my house. Within just the first month of being endowed, I became an ordinance worker in the Provo Temple. I felt most like myself when I was there. Strength and answers and inspiration come from there. I'd look in the mirrors there and couldn't help but smile. I could see how God sees me. Being in the temple is when I felt the most beautiful. I could feel how God felt about me, and I felt unstoppable.

Working in the temple has been one of the biggest blessings of my life. It changed me. I hope you never pass up the opportunity to work in the Lord's house. I loved seeing everyone of all ages wearing white and seeing everyone who came in—whether they were there every week or if it was their first time back in a long time. I loved seeing others' efforts to do more and be better. Just their presence impacted me in a way I don't have words adequate enough to express. I could see and *feel* just a sliver of how Heavenly Father saw and felt about them, and it was overwhelming. I felt that He knew they were there, and He was so proud of them. I knew how proud He was of every single one of them for turning to Him and trying. And I could feel Him smiling at them for their efforts.

"But, Al, isn't the temple a little weird the first time you go?" Let me just shake you now and yell, "No!" You're going to the Lord's house; don't be nervous. It is filled with nothing but the Spirit. When people speak to those who haven't gone to the temple yet, I think they focus too much on the whole "it's so different" phrase that it freaks people out for no reason. Don't get freaked out. Sure, it's different, in a sense that we don't do this in church, but you will be surprised at how comfortable you are there and how strongly you will feel a familiarity with everything. You can know that it is in fact the Lord's literal house, and He does walk those hallways. He knows when you are there, and you can feel it. If things don't make sense to you the first time, isn't that a witness that it is not from man? Don't get confused or discouraged; take confidence knowing that spiritual things come directly from God, not man. The experience will be new but oh so exciting!

"What if I'm afraid of making more promises to God?"

Good. Keep it that way, because you will always be conscious to live the right way. But don't let it stop you from going and making those covenants. The promises you make in the temple are nothing you can't do, and truth be told, you're promising to do things you're probably already *willing* to do had you known what they were before you went.

If you are like me and are seeking to go through the temple outside of preparing for a mission or marriage, His timing truly is best, even if it is devastating to wait. The Spirit often speaks to us with reccurring thoughts. If this is something that keeps coming to your mind, it is definitely time to start taking that thought seriously. Don't let your age or anything else discourage you. The decision to go through the temple is between you, your bishop, and the Lord. In my opinion, the best way to prepare to go to the temple is to be ready and willing to accept everything you will learn and experience there. When you get to the point of knowing that the temple is the house of the Lord and that everything you do and hear there is of God, then you are ready. Many of you will go to the temple because you "have" to go in preparation for a mission or marriage—get excited!

How can you best prepare to go to the temple? There are tons of scriptures you can probably read, but to be honest, scriptures related to the temple didn't make much sense to me until *after* I had gone through the temple and *then* read them. Even now, every time I read in any of the standard works, from the Bible to the Doctrine and Covenants, I am surprised how much the temple is laced in. But the best way to prepare for the temple is to strengthen your testimony. The stronger your testimony is, the more ready you will be, and the more understanding and accepting and receptive you will be to the spiritual things of God. Simple as that.

"Is a temple marriage really something I need to do?"

Yes, please make it a must. There are plenty of little quirks that we can overlook and learn to love and adore in an imperfect being, but anything that jeopardizes covenants are most definitely not those things to overlook. Though we are all familiar with hearing about forever families, we don't often really think about the sad reality of " 'til death do you part." Perhaps we love the idea of being with our spouse forever because it sounds romantic, but a temple marriage is not just there to be cute. It's essential. We cannot receive the highest celestial glory without it. If we choose against getting sealed we are choosing against being exalted and living with God.

When we are sealed, we are sealed not just to our spouse but also to Christ.

I often read emails or hear stories of people who are worried that their tattoos will prevent them from being able to go to the temple. I hope all of this eases your mind. It is God's house, and God does not see our tattoos—not when we've changed and repented, turned to Him, and moved forward.

The temple has blessed literally every aspect of my life. When I went through the temple, I was going on more than three years without hearing from my dad. The day I was endowed, my dad called me out of nowhere. And since that day back in 2012, I have heard from my dad every day. I felt kind of like Abraham when he was asked to give up his only son. When Abraham finally made the decision and committed to put God first no matter what, he was blessed to have Isaac back.

I don't think it's any coincidence at all that it worked out the way that it did. I don't doubt at all that it was a direct blessing from putting God first and doing what He asked me to do, no matter the challenges. And I don't doubt that had I chosen to quit or slow down or take a break in the gospel that I wouldn't have gotten my father back when I did. Whether it was three years later, thirty years later, or in the next lifetime, I'm certain that wouldn't have happened if I didn't continually choose God.

Though I waited for those blessings for years, for others it may be several more years or perhaps after this life that their blessings come. But they do come, and they will be better than what we had in mind. That is what happens when we put God first, just like He promised me in 3 Nephi 13:33 all those years ago. He told me that all of my losses would be made up if I trusted Him no matter what. That promise would always be there if I just kept going, even if I was mad or confused and barely getting by. But when my blessing came, things weren't just okay between my dad and I; despite our long distance, we are closer now than when we were before I was baptized. We speak every day on the phone just to talk. I openly tell my dad everything I am doing, places I'm speaking at, things I've learned at church, any and all things gospel related in my life. Though he may not be interested in the Church, he is interested in me.

I don't know what I'd do without the temple and its blessings. It's home. Don't be afraid; fear is not of God. Relax—you're going to the house of the Lord. Go often. Go to feel the Spirit, and don't worry about understanding everything the first time you go. Making and keeping covenants opens the gate to an outpouring of blessings. It should never be viewed as a burden or approached apprehensively. Rather, it should be sought after and embraced with joy and excitement to partake and receive more fully the greatest blessings ever created, not just in the eternities, but here, daily, in mortality.

Chapter 14 . . .
MARRIAGE

> HEAVENLY FATHER DID NOT SHORTCHANGE OR MESS UP ON YOU. Don't stress. You just worry about you and about God. If we are trying and are patient, Heavenly Father will never forget about us or keep us from the best blessings He has to offer.

GROWING UP AS A nonmember in New York definitely gave me a different culture and way of thinking. I never thought about getting married. It was never a goal of mine, and it was never something I dreamed about as a kid. I always figured I'd eventually get married but left it at that. It wasn't until I joined The Church of Jesus Christ of Latter-day Saints that my mind went to marriage. I always joke that I must have swallowed some of the baptism water, because it wasn't until then that marriage became a goal of mine and that my thoughts would wander off to what my future spouse was doing right then.

When I put my two weeks notice in at work and told my coworkers that I was moving to Utah, it quickly became another thing for them to make fun of me for. In addition to locking me in the office and yelling at me for my beliefs, they started making jabs against not just the religion but the culture as a whole. They placed actual bets that I would be married within six months of moving there.

After my baptism, and especially after my move across the country, problems of every kind came flooding into my life, and dating was added to that list. Married within six months? It was an incredibly lonely time in my life, and for a while I was never even considered for a date, let alone marriage, mostly because guys couldn't get past my appearance. And that was really hard. I had just barely moved to Utah against my will (but following God's), and I was living in a new place, not knowing what I was supposed to do there. Those women at the grocery store were pulling their kids away from me, walking the other direction, and giving me dirty looks. I was feeling absolutely and completely alone in too many ways at once.

Guys my age were looking for temple-worthy girls, but because I didn't exactly look temple worthy, they didn't even speak to me. It was the first time that it ever occurred to me that, appearance aside, my life before the Church could stop guys from wanting to not only date but even be friends. I would notice the kind of girls that were getting asked out and began to be afraid, because I didn't look like them or grow up in a strong gospel-centered family. I didn't know how to cook or make my own skirts, and I was afraid that I was going to be forever overlooked.

Holding on to the promise that if I continued to put God first everything else would fall in to place, I decided to stay focused on what really mattered to me, hoping if I did that things would eventually work out how they ought to. If I stayed close to God, He would bless me. So I worried about me and the relationship I *did* have with God. That was definitely a hefty goal, because not worrying about everything else wasn't easy.

I lived on my own with no roommates, just my discount dog, Lucas, and I quickly grew tired of going home to an empty place by myself. On hard days, it was difficult for me to want to leave the house because I didn't feel strong enough to handle the rude stares. But I also didn't want to stay home in the quiet emptiness of the house, left alone with my thoughts that usually spiraled down into a dance with the adversary. I was so familiar with that dance that I didn't even step on Satan's toes while doing it, all while trying to fight off his attacks on my self-worth.

But I knew that if the Lord helped me before, He would help me again. Sometimes Heavenly Father is all we have, but in all things He is all we need. Because I had decided to always keep going and stay as close to the Lord as I could (even if it was with a lot of tears), things started to unravel in ways I never would have expected. I learned lessons I couldn't imagine living life without. I grew beyond what I thought I could in such a short time, experiencing incredible things and becoming better and stronger.

Because I was speaking so often on top of working full time, I gave up my only date nights, Saturdays, to serve God in His house. I would sit in the celestial room of the temple during my shifts and see girls younger than I was, married, nestled with their husbands, and I couldn't help but be reminded that that wasn't me and probably wouldn't be for a long time.

When I was newly baptized and finally started to think about getting married, I had generic expectations for my future husband: "I want someone tall who can make me laugh."

But really, that's not what was truly most important to me. There were plenty of tall, funny people, but what I wanted most of all was a spiritual attraction. There were things spiritually I needed in a spouse that could not be overlooked. Whoever he was, his most important relationship shouldn't be with me but with God. I needed someone equally spiritual, if not stronger than I was, who could strengthen and help me on my weak days (because I have plenty of those). I needed someone who could fully accept me, my goals, and my independence—someone who could completely accept where I came from and help me get to where I wanted to go in life with the gospel.

The more time passed, the more disheartened I became. Was I expecting too much in a future companion? Was I being too picky? Did the person I need and want even exist? If not, what was I willing to compromise on? Would someone fully accept who I was and who I used to be? Could they accept things I couldn't do and embrace the things I could?

Before the Church announced that technology could be used by missionaries, they piloted the program in several missions. One of those missions was Rochester, where I'm from, as well as the Pennsylvania Philadelphia Mission. Missionaries in those missions were allowed to use Facebook to find and teach people. A lot of the Philadelphia missionaries added me as a friend online because of my blogs and videos. I often spoke to one elder in particular for two reasons: (1) he had an investigator who was going through struggles similar to mine, and (2) because I had a desk job where the word *boring* didn't even come close to describing what it was like there.

We would talk daily about the gospel, and it was a great way to bring the Spirit into my more-than-mundane job. Then he started to forward his weekly emails to me. Then we would send short video messages back and forth to each other. This went on for about a year, all while I was dating, yelling at Heavenly Father over loneliness, and doing that all-too-familiar dance with the adversary.

I never once thought anything would come from those online chats about the Atonement and how cool God was. To be honest, if I knew that he lived so close to me, I wouldn't have spoken to him as often as I did because of the pressure it would have brought me to hang out when he got home and to like him. I spoke to him out of boredom. I'm not sure he can say the same, though. (I later found out he would pray and write in his journal about me. Cute, right?)

I always thought I was expecting too much in someone and that I'd eventually have to settle with some qualities. Then years later, this guy popped up out of nowhere, it seemed! I got a call one night from an Elder Carraway. The elder that I spoke to online for so long called me *right after* he was released as a missionary.

I answered to hear a familiar voice: "Do you know who this is?" I could hear his smile through the phone.

Ben and I hung out a day later. I really wasn't thinking too much about it, and I didn't even know it was a date (which is what he was thinking it was). Had I known that, I wouldn't have picked him up and taken him to the Salt Lake Temple to do a session with me. (Some first date, right?) I strongly believe everyone who can should go and experience a live session. He hadn't been before, so I was going to be the one to bring him—as friends. When we went to get steak afterward, I knew I was in trouble. Two things I love in life are the temple and a good steak. Yeah, I was in trouble.

We clicked just right. Everything I was afraid of with myself and my life—normally quick deal breakers for so many—were never even a red flag to Ben (or a yellow flag, for that matter). There we were eating steak, and he was talking about himself in this constant flow of word vomit in the most fascinating and exciting way ever. I remember realizing that we had too many goals and similarities than I cared to tell him about for a while. I didn't want to be the crazy girl who, after just a few dates, says that he reminds her of her patriarchal blessing. I just sat there, listened, smiled, and probably gave him some weird facial expressions while I was internally connecting so many dots from him to me and thinking, *Uh-oh.*

After his homecoming talk (which was the second time we had seen each other), Ben asked if I wanted to see where things could go. I told him we couldn't be official because he needed to date other people. He didn't like that answer. He told me he had dated enough before his mission. I liked that answer because I really didn't want him to date other people; it just logically made sense to me. So that was that.

From the day he got home from his mission, Ben really cannonballed into this different lifestyle because of me. We hung out almost daily. During our first week of dating, I was on the cover of *LDS Living* Magazine for two months, and my most popular blog post, "Tattooed Mormon," was released, reaching over a million views in just half a day. I'm not sure he realized that he would walk out of the frozen food section of the grocery store and turn into the designated picture taker when people recognized me. Within the first month of meeting each other in person, we traveled to four different states together because of my speaking schedule. Every day, whether in Utah or not, we would spend hours together in the car, traveling to my firesides, just talking. We joke, saying we had a car courtship. If you want to really get to know someone, I have two words for you: *road trip.*

I mean, let's face it, I'm no different than anyone else. I am filled with flaws, awkwardness, breakdowns, sass, and setbacks. But regardless of my flaws, Ben seemed to never run out of patience and willingness with me. My speaking schedule led him to live a life I'm sure he wouldn't have initially picked for himself: sacrificing his free time, passing up a hike or a new restaurant or movies and even his siblings' birthday dinners, just spending all his extra time in a car driving to who-knows-where with me. Not only was he patient and willing with my schedule, but he also accepted my independence and drive to do more and help more.

Due to fears from past relationships, I had set weird timelines in my head. I wanted to date someone for at least two years before I ever *thought* about bringing up marriage. But despite that, we met, dated, got engaged, and then got married and sealed in the Oquirrh Mountain Temple all within six months. But honestly, once Heavenly Father lets you know that something is right, even six months seems too long to wait.

I honestly believe that Ben came as a blessing in response to my efforts with the Lord. And part of me believes jokingly (but not really) that it came from sacrificing my date night to be in the temple. Because of Ben, his testimony, and those qualities that were important to me, we find we work better as a team than we ever did on our own, and hard things in life are easier. I'm so grateful that I was patient enough to wait to meet him. I hate to think what life would be like if I hadn't been patient. I hate to think of life without our experiences, laughs, and lessons, and our daughter, Gracie. I hate to think what I would have missed if I didn't trust God. The truth is, I'm not sure what kind of wife I'd be without the qualities and lessons and talents I developed while I was single and "waiting." I am such a better person because of them.

I once saw a question online that asked, "What's the one thing that brings you the most joy?"

And I thought, *Easy, my husband.* Then, *Wait . . . No—God . . . Wait . . .*

And as I was thinking (probably much more deeply than was intended), I realized how perfectly Heavenly Father has blessed me with Ben, whom He uses hundreds of times every day to help and bless me and answer my prayers. I'm grateful for God and His ways and His all-knowing eye and guidance in my life. I'm nothing without God. And I'm incredibly grateful for my husband, his strengths, passion, humor, patience, and presence in my life. But I'm mostly grateful for the love and joy he has on his own for God; that truly makes what we have incredible.

That's what marriage should be: a team to make the journey back to God easier and more fulfilling. Do hard things together. *Always* have time for love. Help each other reach goals. Every day make one-on-one time to just talk. Hold hands when you pray. But mostly, seek the Lord *together* and make the temple the centerpiece of your lives. The most important relationship we will ever have is with our Heavenly Father, but through Him all other relationships in our life will strengthen.

If you haven't been already, you will be blessed with a companion who will help you in the ways you need, even if sometimes you feel like that person doesn't exist or you're asking for too much or you're too picky. Don't allow passing time to bring doubt or cause you to settle. Don't lose patience and miss out on what He has in store for you. And in the meantime, don't hold yourself back from learning and growing and experiencing other things. Just hold on, and don't lose confidence. Heavenly Father knows what's important to us and what we need.

Don't waste your thoughts comparing yourself and defining yourself by what you aren't and others are. Don't allow yourself to question, "What is wrong with me?" Heavenly Father did not shortchange or mess up on you. Don't stress. You just worry about you and worry about God. If we are trying and are patient, Heavenly Father will *never* forget about us or keep us from the best blessings He has to offer.

Sure, our future can be uncertain at times, but how exciting that is! How exciting it is to know we're guided by God!

Happiness and unhappiness exist in every situation; different people have different experiences. It's true—life is what you make it. Or it could be what you *allow* God to make of it for you. What will you choose?

We cannot afford to let God be an afterthought. Though, when we remember who He really is, I can't think of any reason we wouldn't want Him at the center of our lives. Today and every day, choose happiness. To choose happiness is to choose God. Choose to keep going. Choose to trust. Choose to have faith, to keep your hope. Be happy and stay patient. Live and love today. Choose to receive the unexpected but profoundly greater path with the best blessings. I promise, you'll be all right.

Chapter 15 . . .
YOUR WORTH

> You are GOOD ENOUGH,
> and GOD DOES CARE.

MORE OFTEN THAN I care to admit, I feel inadequate with what I'm doing. I feel like giving up, and I doubt my efforts. I feel like what I'm doing doesn't make a difference and that the extra mile doesn't matter and goes unnoticed.

Because, really, who am I? I am no different than anybody else. I'm awkward, I'm silly, I'm weak, I stumble, and I often fall short.

Every day I receive hate mail and hurtful comments on my posts. I am told daily that I'm a bad person. I've heard everything, including, "You're wrong," "Your life is a joke," "You look like a disaster," "Your efforts are a failure," "You shouldn't be allowed to go to church or the temple looking the way you do," "There's no way God could love someone like you," and even "You should take your own life because the world would be better without you and your terrible example." And these comments and emails are coming from active members of the Church.

I don't understand why it's so hard to be respectful on social media (and in general). I don't know why it's so hard to notice and praise people's efforts, even if those efforts seem small to us. Why are we so quick to point out their wrongdoings and even quicker to comment about it publicly on their pages? Why are we so slow to help, uplift, and build up?

Saying "I'm not judging, but . . ." *is* judging and is *so* hurtful and destructive to even the "strongest" of people. There will never be a single reason that justifies negativity toward anyone, especially those you don't know, even if you are "just saying." Please, think before commenting online. If that is something you struggle with, please help by not commenting at all. The adversary is on all of us enough as it is—let's not add any more weight to someone's day or self-worth.

I'm not looking for pity by saying this. My point is that no matter who you are, no matter what you look like, no matter what you have (or don't have), no matter what you are trying to do, opposition will come. It will always be there.

Do not listen to it.

Don't let opposition drag you down. Do not let Satan win. Do not let people stop you from trying, from succeeding, and from making a difference. What we do matters, and the rest of eternity depends on how we react and live. Life really is an incredible journey, and we only get to do this mortal thing once. Stay focused on what truly matters. Don't waste your life dwelling on and believing the bad. Don't let negative comments and remarks (even from members of the Church) slow you down. Look for the good and delete the bad.

But mostly, do not be the one who holds you back.

The day I decided to be baptized was the day my elders were going to drop me as an investigator. They were going to stop teaching me. Why? I was right there, I was so close, that exact day. Why would they do that?

They thought they weren't making a difference. They thought that maybe someone else could teach me better: maybe someone who had read the Book of Mormon all the way through or who had a stronger testimony, someone more confident or outgoing or popular, maybe someone who dressed better, someone who was better at sports, someone who didn't struggle as much before their mission or who left for their mission on time. My elders thought that because of their supposed shortcomings, someone else would be more effective than they were. That's what they thought.

But little did they know, right? Little did they know that just by them trying, regardless of what they *thought* their shortcomings were, I'm here. I am here, doing everything that I'm doing, and I'm happy—full of that real and lasting happiness. Could you imagine if they had quit? Could you imagine if they had let that stop them? Where would I be? I don't know.

And I don't want to know.

And little do *you* know the profound impact that you have and will continue to have on those around you, even on those you will never meet, just by trying, by you being you. Because the best thing we could ever be is ourselves.

It should never be about what you don't know or can't do. Don't focus on what you don't have and what others do. Do not be ashamed or embarrassed with who you are or what you look like. And more than anything, do not think you cannot do this. What you know and what you have is enough for His help and guidance, and He will help you to be your best self, to succeed, and to have an impact on so many others.

Of course we are being used. Of course He needs us. And of course we are different. We have to be different to help different people in different ways, in such perfect ways that we can't even understand right now.

One of the biggest things people struggle with is comparison. Why? Why do we do that? Why do we pick ourselves apart? Why do we spend our thoughts and emotions on what we don't like and wish we could change about ourselves or the things we aren't doing as well as others or aren't doing at all? Why do we define ourselves by what we can't do or don't have?

Your worth is already established: it is infinite, and that will not change. But the problem isn't that we don't know our self-worth; it is that we have a hard time remembering it with all the outside influences in our lives—speaking the loudest through social media. My husband told me once that there is a reason we have two ears: Satan yells in one, and the Spirit whispers in the other.

I believe that the secret to having your best life is fully accepting who you are and loving it. To fully accept yourself, you have to understand and love how God sees you. Our perfect Creator created you perfectly—perfectly different from anyone else. Being different is crucial and incredible! The Lord needs you to be *you*, not someone else. He needs our differences, our talents, and our quirks; how could His plan work if we were all the same?

Love everyone, including yourself.

Comparing yourself to someone else doesn't help you be better. Your goals and efforts to being *your* best self should be based on doing your best, not someone else's. The only person we should compare ourselves to is who we were yesterday.

One time I did an interview on BYU Radio, speaking on this very matter, and I loved the segment that aired right before I went on: "Treat yourself the way you treat others" (Maddy Richards). You don't point out their flaws and tell them everything they are horrible at. You don't tell them what you think is ugly or what you wish they could change. "We lift, appreciate, and accept others and help them, and we need to start doing that for ourselves as well," she said.

God does not define you by your faults or shortcomings but by your heart and potential. But would you rather hear it from me or from the Lord? Sometimes I still struggle with this. I read over those words and think, "Yeah, I know it, but how can I *feel* it?"

Heavenly Father weeps when we don't see ourselves the way He sees us. Ask the Lord to see yourself as He sees you—you will receive a sure knowledge that you are beautiful. Actually do this. Ask Him in prayer to see yourself the way He sees you, because that is the secret to having your best life: seeing yourself the way God sees you and *knowing* it. Next time you look in the mirror, look longer and deeper. Confidence and comfort can always be there because Christ and Heavenly Father will always be there to show you, and "he loveth our souls" (Alma 24:14).

Wayne Dyer shared the well-known story of a grandfather talking to his grandson about two wolves fighting inside of him. The first wolf is filled with anger, hatred, bitterness, and mostly revenge. The second wolf is filled with love, kindness, compassion, and mostly forgiveness. "Which wolf do you think will win?" the young boy inquired. The grandfather responded, "Whichever one I feed."

Our bodies or income don't define who we are; God sees what's inside us, and that is what matters to Him. When we listen to negative comments, we're giving permission and allowing the adversary in. When life gets me down, it's only because I allow it to. Don't allow it anymore. Do not feed the adversary's "wolf"; don't keep it alive any longer. Don't seek others' attention or praise.

Your life doesn't have to be out of a magazine. Your pictures don't have to be professionally taken, and you don't need all these editing apps and filters. Don't waste your thoughts comparing yourself and defining yourself by what you aren't and what others are. No matter who you are, no matter what you look like, and no matter your calling, your house, your wardrobe, the number of followers you have, the quality of your photos, or your salary—there will always be someone there to knock you down several pegs. Don't take it personally, and please do not listen. It is happening to every single one of us. So chin up! You just be you, because that is the best thing you could ever be. How incredibly sad it will be if we don't make it back to Him, especially because of an untrue jab from someone who wasn't thinking.

Don't ever feel inadequate—that's the adversary. Do not be ashamed of who you are. Refrain from thinking what you do doesn't make a difference. Refrain from thinking someone else could do it better. Refrain from thinking you are not being supported, that you are inadequate in any degree. Learn to be less self-critical, because you are so beautiful in the eyes of God. His thoughts toward you are more numerous than you can even begin to imagine. You are not overlooked, not even for a second.

I have met a ton of people—all different with very different situations and experiences—but in everyone's life, it's the same Christ, the same Heavenly Father, the same love. Neither of Them loves me more or less than They love anyone else, no more or less than they love you. No matter who you are, no matter where in life you are, no matter what you've done or are not doing, no matter your sins or accomplishments, no matter income or calling, no matter if you're on or off the path—the love They have for you, personally and individually, is always there, always strong, and always real. The love They have for you *specifically* never wavers or dims. I have felt that so consistently and so overwhelmingly that I can't adequately express or describe it in words.

Someone once asked me a general question, and usually general questions are the hardest to answer. I was asked, "With all of the experiences you've had with speaking and blogging, what has been the most consistent thing you have seen or learned?"

I thought, *Holy cow, I've learned something new and vital every day from everywhere and everyone, so how can I answer that? I have been consistently humbled by all the places I've traveled to, all the opportunities that have arisen, and all the people I have been able to meet, all which have taught me many, many things. How am I supposed to answer to this?*

The answer came to me as I pondered this scenario: "If this were the last time I ever got to speak to them, if this were the last thing I ever got to say, and if this were the last they ever saw me or heard from me, what would I most want them to know?"

As I was pondering and reading through my journals on everything I've felt and struggled with and learned, my answer came from a powerful experience I had a few years ago. I was supposed to speak at a girls' camp on a night when I had the worst migraine you could imagine. It was so bad, it brought me to tears. I couldn't even think straight, let alone go and speak for an hour. It was absolutely terrible. I was praying (well, more screaming than saying a prayer) to Heavenly Father, telling Him I couldn't do this, there was no way, not tonight, not feeling like this. I was going to cancel. I didn't want to go. The response back from God didn't seem to come right then, but the next thing I knew, I found myself driving through a canyon to girls' camp. As I was talking to Heavenly Father on the way there, I received an answer I hadn't received while I was sitting in my car in my driveway, yelling at Him. The answer came so clearly that it was like I was reading a billboard, so powerfully that I physically felt it. I was consumed. I was taken over. I was crying, except this time it wasn't because of my head, but because of my answer.

Heavenly Father answered my prayer, saying, "Al, you go tonight. You go and make sure that you tell those girls how much I love them. Al, go to those girls and tell them that I notice them, that I'm listening. You make sure you tell those girls that I'm right here."

I got goose bumps. I'm getting goose bumps just writing it. It came so clearly that I responded out loud, in tears, "Okay, I'll tell them!"

Embrace yourself. Love what you can do and accept what you can't. Love your differences, and most important, be proud of yourself! Love who you are and where you are. Don't spend your time looking ahead, pleading for things to be over or different. Stop looking backward. Stop yearning and waiting for the future. Today, where you are right now, is a joy. Today, right now, is the best place to be. Happiness, opportunities, and blessings do await us in *this* day.

Among the things you don't have or can't do, one thing you *do* have that you can't trade for anything is a knowledge that Heavenly Father is yours and loves, listens, and helps you regardless of your flaws or shortcomings.

That is what matters most. If this is the only time you ever hear from me, if this is the only thing you know, I plead with you to know that God loves you so much! Know that this is all real. It's as real as your heart beating right now. It's powerful. And you can always feel that when you ask Him and look a little deeper and longer.

What I have truly come to learn and feel and *know* to be very true is that God *does* care. No one goes unnoticed. *You* are not unnoticed, not for a second. This exact second, God is mindful of you. And the second after that, and all the seconds after those. What I have truly come to learn and re-learn, to feel and re-feel, is that you do matter. May I be so bold as to tell you something your Father in Heaven wants you to know? He needs you to know how much you matter to Him, that He loves you just as you are. When He thinks of you, He smiles.

Exist to be happy, not impress. Don't lose sight of why we are here and what we need to be doing and striving toward. Don't lose sight of what is most important. If it doesn't matter, get rid of it. The greatest thing you can ever have and share is your testimony, and you'll make the biggest impact when you are fully and completely yourself. Quit worrying over things that don't matter. Just relax, enjoy life, and enjoy being completely true to who you are.

Hey, you. Be kind to yourself. Be proud of yourself, because you matter. What you do matters. You make a difference. You really are good enough, pretty enough, and strong enough. You are worth it. You do deserve the best. You *do* deserve to be happy, always. Do not hold yourself back any longer, because great things await you, just as you are. Strive every day to be a little better, to be the best you. Believe in yourself and believe in God.

Keep going. Keep trying. Keep doing good. And keep smiling, because you truly are so great. I need you. The world needs you, just as you are. We need you and your uniqueness and your efforts, because you make this a better place. You inspire me even with your messy house, your loud kids, and your bad-quality photos. You are so beautiful. You are doing an incredible job. You are loved by so many and always loved by God. Thank you for being you.

Chapter 16 . . .

LIFE IS *OH* *SO* GOOD

> Forget not that you have a GOD, and HE IS YOURS! He is yours to keep and yours to turn to—ALWAYS.

"I know that I am nothing; as to my strength I am weak; therefore I will not boast of myself, but I will boast of my God, for in his strength I can do all things" (Alma 26:12).

SO HERE I AM, living in Arizona, writing a book, having just celebrated our daughter's first birthday, still uncertain what God has up His sleeve and what will unfold for me next. It's wild to see how my life has worked out since I made the decision to trust and never quit. My life is not at all what I planned or expected; it's profoundly better.

Not once have things gone the way I had in mind, not once. And that can be hard, especially in prayer—and when you think they're righteous, good things you're asking for and they mean so much to you. That is when we have those fleeting thoughts of, *Does God care? Does He really care about me? Is He even there still? Does He even exist at all?*

But how grateful I am! How grateful I am that life did not go the way I had in mind. My life has been *profoundly* better than what I ever imagined it would be and greater than I even knew existed! And I love that.

Life is oh so good. The gospel makes it incredible.

I look back at those nights I spent screaming on the floor, yelling at God, "I can't do this! This is too hard, I'm not this strong!"; those times when I asked where He was or why nothing was coming together yet; those moments when I was brought down to desperately low levels of anguish that I had never before felt. What amazing blessings! Every single one of those times brought me to where I am now and closer to God. Every single one of those times brought me greater understanding and opportunities and blessings. Without *those* times and without Him, I wouldn't have a single thing I have now. The best thing you could ever do for yourself and your family is obey God.

The lessons I have learned are priceless. I can't imagine going any further in life without these lessons and experiences. Every bit of pain, confusion, discomfort, and loneliness weren't for nothing; they were for the best, a 1,000 percent worth it. As hard as things were and continue to be, I am happy. Through all of that, that happiness has *not once* left but has gotten stronger and stronger.

I am overwhelmed with happiness, that lasting and real happiness. I'm not talking about a happiness that comes from just one great thing or one great moment but a happiness that has been lasting and *constant* through all the days, every day, in every situation. This is a heavenly happiness, a gift that is always available to us when we put God first, no matter what, even with uncertainties or trials.

Lovin' this life of mine, not because it's easy or perfect, because it's not, but because it's handpicked by God. This is it. This is my life. Christ is my life. And I refuse to give up. I won't stop until the whole world realizes how awesome life is with the gospel—with God—and no one takes it for granted.

But it's not about me or my life, is it? No, nor will it ever be.

It's about you.

Though this is a book about my story, it's not ultimately about what I overcame or have become. It's about you, who *you* need to become. It's about the things *you* need to overcome and conquer.

You need to know that there is so much more that I could be doing and I'm not. There are things I am doing that I could be doing *so* much better; I know that. Every day I am reminded of that. But what you *need* to know is that if you just try, your *real* try, you will end up in places you never would have thought, doing things you never would have dreamed, becoming better, becoming the person Heavenly Father has wanted you to become all along. And, oh, what a feeling that is! What a feeling!

Remember, Heavenly Father has *already* prepared all of the blessings we're trying to attain. He already put the time, the love, the work, and the effort into preparing the absolute best ever created just for you. And you can have it if you just try, if you always keep going, if you just put Him first, no matter what.

Yeah, it takes work. It takes effort and courage and faith. Remember, we have everything to lose if we give up. Do not lose confidence or faith. Don't you quit. Don't you dare stop. Don't do it! Giving up is not an option. Life is too short to not love the journey God has for you.

Yeah, it's hard, but that won't change. Hard times will consistently be there, but so will Christ. With Him, we will overcome and conquer absolutely everything—every trial, every addiction, every feeling of sadness, weakness, loneliness, fear, doubt, anxiety, temptation. Everything. With Him we overcome and conquer the world!

Christ died so that we may live, so let us live well.

If we think Heavenly Father will do anything to stop us from returning to Him or from overcoming, we're wrong. If we think He will do anything to stop us from being happy right now, even during our hard times, we are wrong. He loves us. He loves *you*. And when I say *you*, I do not mean us as a whole. I mean *you*, personally and individually you. He loves you so much.

This exact second, God is mindful of you.

Your prayers *have* been heard, and greater things are in store for you. Your future is greater than you knew was an option for yourself, than you even knew existed. And you can have those blessings if you just continue in God.

Our God is an unchangeable God. That doesn't mean just His commandments will not change, but neither will His love. That love is never changing, never weakening, never wavering. It is always there, always strong for you. And you can feel that even in the most confusing and darkest of times if you just turn to Him. We just need to try. We just need to choose to trust and to have faith. Choose God daily, no matter what.

Decide how to react. Decide to be happy today, even in your trials and with other people's shortcomings. Decide to love and be an example rather than judge and scold. Decide to laugh a lot and follow God. Live the gospel and eat lots of pizza. Be a little better than you were yesterday. Exist to be happy, not to impress. Experience forgiveness and extend forgiveness. Don't let a bad day make you feel like you have a bad life. Quit worrying over things that don't matter, because life is too short to not love the journey and lessons God has for you. Just relax, enjoy life, and enjoy it being completely true to who you are and who God wants you to be.

"Ye have not come thus far save it were by the word of Christ with unshaken faith in him, relying wholly upon the merits of him who is mighty to save. Wherefore, ye must press forward with a steadfastness in Christ, having a perfect brightness of hope, and a love of God and of all men. Wherefore, if ye shall press forward, feasting upon the word of Christ, and endure to the end, behold, thus saith the Father: Ye shall have eternal life. And now, behold, my beloved brethren, this is the way; and there is none other way" (2 Nephi 31:19–21).

The gospel is not our last option; it's our only option. *This* is real. What we're doing *is* real. What we're a part of is so real! And it is so great! This is the greatest thing to ever be a part of. If you feel like you do not fit in, you're wrong. This gospel is for *you.* These blessings and promises are for you. You belong here; you are a part of this.

Knowing that God is real and the gospel is true means that your life will never be the same but always better. The incredible thing about the gospel is you're doing things you never thought you could do. Don't worry over things that haven't ever (and may never) happen. Fear should never be an option when we remember who God truly is. Embrace the unexpected, knowing who is guiding you.

Forget not why we are here, what it is you need to be doing, what you are a part of! Forget not whose hands you're in—the best hands. Forget not that *you* have a God and He is yours to keep, yours to turn to! Forget not that you have a God who is always there for *you,* personally and individually. He never leaves but is always there to guide and direct and warn, to give you the best ever created, greater than you can imagine. And I love that.

This is happiness, *real* and lasting happiness that you can physically feel.

Heavenly Father *is* real. I am here because of Him. I am happy because of Him. I am able to keep going because of Him. I don't know what I'd do without Him, and I'm grateful I don't ever have to.

"I know that which the Lord hath commanded me, and I glory in it. I do not glory of myself, but I glory in that which the Lord hath commanded me; yea, and this is my glory, that perhaps I may be an instrument in the hands of God to bring some soul to repentance; and this is my joy" (Alma 29:9).

So now, we do the only things we know how to do. Keep going. Keep trusting Him. See where the Spirit will lead us next. See what lessons we'll learn, the experiences we'll have, the people we'll meet, the states we'll live in, the talents we'll develop, the trials we'll conquer. Try not to yell at God when things don't make sense and when they are so hard. Stay patient and faithful and allow life to unfold the way He would have it. *Allow* ourselves to be continuously prepared for and accepting of the unexpected, knowing that it is guided by the *most* powerful and all-knowing Being to ever exist. He exists for us. He exists for *you*. He exists to see you succeed, be truly happy, and return.

Time is moving at the quickest rate I've ever experienced before, and we can't do anything to slow it down. We just need to keep moving with it in a meaningful way. We only get to do this mortal thing once, and I'd hate to waste it or take it for granted. Today will never happen again. Make it count.

In Doctrine and Covenants 76, Joseph Smith describes the members of the terrestrial kingdom: "These are they who are not valiant in the testimony of Jesus; wherefore, they obtain not the crown over the kingdom of our God" (verse 79). That is my greatest fear—good, honorable people who received a lesser glory simply because they were not productive in their testimony.

We may not have all the answers we want about our future, but we know enough. We are led by an all powerful, all loving God. Why stop when we can keep going? Because can you think of anything more important than eternal life and endless happiness?

With God, life is oh so good. He knows our todays, our tomorrows, and every day of our existence. He already has the way for us to receive the best *ever* created. It's already there. I want that. I choose God, His ways, and His rewards and blessings.

Refuse to be idle and have these quickly passing days without substance or meaning or progress. Refuse to pass through life without God. Don't deny yourself the best things by putting off talking to God or reading scriptures.

Today, with God, you have the power to do anything. What will you choose to do with your time? Every day turn to Him, keep going, and recommit. And every day you will become better, feel happiness, and feel Him close to you.

"Shall we not go on in so great a cause? Go forward and not backward. Courage, brethren; and on, on to the victory!" (D&C 128:22).

Part 3

- Continuing the Story -

New Chapter!

IN TIMES OF DOUBT

> The BLESSINGS in our life, even the hard and unexpected ones, are real blessings, from a REAL GOD, who really does love us, who really did handpick those exact things to help us succeed gloriously, and is preparing a place in heaven for you THIS EXACT MOMENT. No part of that is ordinary or insignificant. I'm not sure how it could make us feel anything but EMPOWERED.

IT'S A PRETTY WILD FEELING being back at my laptop writing something for *More Than the Tattooed Mormon*. Except this time, I'm in Utah. Though my dream was to stay forever in Arizona, Heavenly Father brought us back. We did however, just get back from a visit there and I loved every hot second of it. Ben graduated at ASU with his degree in organizational leadership, and since he did it online, we thought it would be awesome to fly out there for him to walk the stage—not only because it was absolutely a *huge* accomplishment, but also because we'll take any reason to bring us back to Arizona. Ben will do his masters online at Northern Arizona University, and I look forward to when we can fly back for another visit when he graduates then too, if not sooner.

Since the first release of *More Than the Tattooed Mormon*, Ben and I have actually written a book together about dating and marriage, called *Cheers to Eternity*, which was a thrilling experience to do with him! Everything we learned was poured into this thing. It's a whole lot of the funny, the embarrassing, the *honest*, and the uplifting. We wrote this with the intention of it being for singles and newlyweds, but we are so completely surprised that almost all of our feedback, reviews, and comments are from marriage veterans of 20+ years, and *wow* has it been overwhelmingly amazing to read their responses!

We are surprised and humbled to hear so many of you driven to change to make life better! *Cheers to Eternity* isn't an advice book. It isn't us telling you how to live. It isn't us giving the answers in bullet points. But it is us opening up. It is us talking about important and hard things. It is us telling you our failures. Our lessons. And it is very much us promoting making the time to be together and be happy. It's about looking and creating the good and the exciting. It's about searching for and loving God together. It's about being productive in trials. It's about coming together and strengthening. It's about not taking anything for granted and making sure our spouse is respected and treated like the best friend they were when we said, *I Do*. It's the reminder that we can live however we want! We don't have to let others dictate the way we live.

It's about remembering what God has brought us and taking advantage of it so we can flourish! Because we believe that marriage is of God. And all things God asks us to do are to help us and to make us be *happy*. Because isn't it so true that, in general, our biggest downfall in life is not fully realizing what we have and taking things for granted? (And it may or may not also be about Ben's bad jokes and several references to *The Office*).

And also, *wow* to my mom. My non-member, sixty-year-old, divorced mom, who read our book and said, "I gotta tell you . . . if I had your new book back in the day . . . it would have saved our marriage." If she can be impacted by our book, I'm excited at the possibility of others who can to be too. If you go read *Cheers to Eternity*, we definitely wouldn't be mad at you, haha.

We welcomed another blondie to our family: Christian. He is the most inquisitive little boy, nicknamed the King of Smolder. He and Gracie are inseparable. We have a goal to be outside as much as we can and see how many National Parks we can visit together.

My sister Rachel and Scott are still married and just welcomed their third child.

My discount dog, Lucas, recently passed away, but somehow, we managed to find an even bigger and more doofy dog that we brought into our family. We rescued Gatsby, though appropriately nicknamed "Fat-sby," from a Vegas shelter.

I'm going against my book aesthetics to add this picture in here. This is Dad Fox. I know most of you are probably wondering about him and us. Every year, we travel back to New York to visit my family. I never visited home until Gracie was born (mostly because I didn't have funds to do so). I'm adding this for all those who may have family members who don't approve of your decision to get baptized. I know the heartache and confusion and loneliness and silence that comes from that.

So, this picture is a little somethin' somethin' as proof that you don't have to sacrifice Church membership for things to improve with your family. And this picture is proof that losses can be made up, miracles still happen, relationships can mend, all is not lost, trials are not lasting, things do get better, and God is most definitely in charge.

Sometimes it takes long years, like me. Sometimes much longer. But when we don't sacrifice living the gospel and we continue to put God first, regardless of the trials, the best blessings always come. When we choose to trust God, especially through heartache and confusion, we will never be shortchanged from the absolute best ever created.

And me? I'm still me. I'm still speaking a lot, still writing a lot, still awkward, still telling jokes no one laughs at, and still eating too many tacos. At age twenty-nine, I earned my Young Women's medallion, and my convert heart is elated!

It was a lot of work, but we make time for whatever it is we prioritize and deem important. Few things in life are worth so much dedication while proving to be life changing. But after finally finishing the Personal Progress program, I believe this is 100% one of them. If you haven't done it yet, do it! Age does not matter. Being a convert or not does not matter. Whatever your calling is (I'm *not* in Young Women's) does not matter. I asked my bishop what things need to happen to get started, and he said all you need to do is let your bishop know and he'll get you going! Your soul will thank you!

It's always amazing to look back and see how things worked out, where we ended up, how we've grown, and what has changed. I'm looking back from where I was when I first wrote this book several years ago, and I find great gratitude in the unexpected that brought me to everything I have now.

I still continue to go through great trials, some much harder than what I even wrote in here, and I still find myself yelling at God sometimes because of the weight and fatigue I am feeling from them. I've gone through a whole slew of things from death, to long-term unemployment, to surgeries and car accidents. And although in the moment the suffering is *very* real and *very* difficult, it's also a little silly in hindsight, because it is those exact situations when I was yelling at God and wondering where He was that have brought me to *everything* I have now. And it breaks my heart to imagine my life being any different than what it is!

Right around the time this book was first released, I unexpectedly lost my job. Ben was a full-time student still, I just found out I was pregnant with Christian, and we were living in the middle of nowhere in Arizona. And when I say in the middle of nowhere, I mean the only thing in our city was basically just a Family Dollar and a whole lot of cotton fields. Despite our best efforts every day, nothing worked out for us. It was nine months of searching, fasting, praying, pleading, losing my voice, living off of our savings account, and still having no job. That's a terrible situation for anyone to be in, and just a little more terrible when you have a family to support. And just a little more terrible when you're pregnant with no insurance, and no money to go to the doctors. I had such a heavy weight thinking of our financial situation, and an even heavier weight (which actually seemed more like a sickness the way that it affected me) was not knowing whether our baby was healthy or not. What I would have given just to hear his heartbeat!

I didn't think this trial could have affected us anymore negatively than it already did. I vividly remember telling Ben just months previous how Arizona just had its way with me and that "if Heavenly Father would let me, I'd stay here forever." But this trial came, and the time kept passing, and it ended up ripping me away from the state I so desperately love.

I feel like I handled the situation with grace and faith when it first presented itself. I'm by nature an optimist; I was hopeful and happy even. I saw it as a great opportunity, actually, even though it was a surprise. But then the months kept passing and nothing had improved—things only worsened. I felt like I had been faithful for long enough that I should have *earned* it to end by now as my reward. Did your eyes roll reading that? Mine did typing it. But it was definitely how I felt. We may have faith to be helped or healed right then and there, but do we have the faith to *not* be?

At this time, I was rolling my eyes at the thought of the New Year that approached. How much of it was really a "new, fresh start" when I was bringing this same, heavy trial along with me into it. But no matter how dim things seemed, and no matter how much time had passed, one night when I was all out of tears to cry and my body ached from stress and fatigue, God spoke peace to me. But it wasn't during the time I was yelling at Him wondering where He was. And it wasn't during the time I was pleading for things to be over or things to be different. It was the time where I was laying on the floor in prayer, exhausted, in silence. Listening.

God reminded me of the talk by Elder Holland about Lot's wife. Elder Holland said, "She doubted the Lord's ability to give her something better than she already had. Apparently she thought—fatally, as it turned out—that nothing that lay ahead could possibly be as good as those moments she was leaving behind. . . . Faith trusts that God has great things in store for each of us." (Jeffrey R. Holland, "'Remember Lot's Wife': Faith Is for the Future" (Brigham Young University devotional, Jan. 13, 2009), speeches.byu.edu.)

Then my soul was pierced with energy as I read of Elder Holland's wife grabbing him by the collars—at a time where they, too, were questioning their situation, their future, their finances, and giving up—as she looked him square in the eye and spoke boldly, "the future holds *everything* for us." My heart started to race and I felt this jolt of energy run through my body, but it wasn't energy, it was my soul coming *alive* for the first time in months, it seemed. It was almost as if God Himself was grabbing *me* by the collars, looking *me* in the eyes, and telling me boldly that truly, *the future holds everything for us.*

The trial eventually passed. It was a text book definition of eleventh-hour blessing. We only had thirty dollars left in our account and were living off of my in-law's food storage when our first paycheck came. Since then, we've built up our bank account, had a healthy baby, and found a job that has been perfect for us in a location that has (I hate to admit) also been perfect for us for the season we are in now. And it wasn't necessarily a "happily ever after," because it wasn't long after that a *different something* to overcome came along. But, of course, things worked out better than they were before the trial even came. I say *of course* because when we remember who God really is, and His purpose, *of course* He will always bring us to best things. That's what He does. His whole purpose is to help us succeed.

Sometimes it's easier to see that when *other* people are in a trial, rather than ourselves. A good friend of mine also had to relocate with her family to an undesirable place. As an outsider looking in, I'm not sure why she was having that hard a time, I would have *loved* to live in their new home, it was gorgeous *and* in Arizona. But she hated it and admitted to crying every day for the first month. I remember thinking, *how can you be this upset when you don't even know what's right around the corner? How can you be this upset when you don't even know what will come from this and what it will lead to?* Ah, if only I had those calm thoughts during my trial. We may be in a hard season right now, but seasons don't last forever. And we may be blinded by the unexpected and held down by the weight of the unwanted, but we don't know what's right around the corner for us. It is, *of course,* guided by a perfect God. And because of that, the future holds *everything* for us.

I think it's common for us all to have doubts creep in—either from a trial or from lack of efforts on our end, or maybe just silly fleeting ones that come when your mind wanders during a menial task. I totally have random and fleeting doubts sometimes.

Just recently I was vacuuming my living room and as I was vacuuming, I realized I just spent a good five minutes entertaining the idea of: *What if this is all in our heads? What if this isn't true? What if we made ourselves believe this because it sounds nice? What if all my efforts within the gospel don't matter and I really can live however I want? What if there's not really any way to know what comes next? What if all of this is for nothing?*

It's interesting, living in the time that we do.

Who knew how easy it would be to be influenced by the confusion and the hurt of the world? How dictating the worldly trends could be with our time? Who knew how damaging the distractions of good things are to keep us from the best things? Who knew just how easy it would be to over complicate enduring? Who knew the subtleties of the adversary could be so damaging, and yet so hard to pick up on sometimes?

But these doubts, they don't take away from the truthfulness of the gospel. And these fleeting, yet sometimes heavy, doubts cannot take away from what I felt when I got confirmed a member of the Church. Those fleeting doubts, no matter how crafty from the adversary, cannot take away from what I felt when I did temple work for all four of my grandparents. And my aunt. And my uncle. *Goosebumps.*

Nothing can take away from what I felt just last week at church during someone's testimony when they recited the First Vision and said, without blinking, *"Hear Him."* Or last month when I was one of the speakers at a two-day conference at a completely packed convention center. Two days where I watched while *ten thousand* of you sang in unison and prayed and laughed and cried together and opened up and talked about God. What I felt that weekend was real. It was physical. It changed me. And even with my long, tiring trials, I have had too many moments where my body was completely consumed with the undeniable reality that God is with us. And it *jolted* my *soul* to *dance* within me!

These moments, though sometimes rare, are so real. When you experience them and remember them, try and tell yourself the Church isn't true. And that God isn't real. I dare you. You can't. And *that* is why I'm here still. That is why I keep going, even during those really hard trials that will consistently be there in our life.

Time and time again, I have these indescribable feelings where I have felt my soul *dancing* within me! Those goose-bump, soul-dancing, heart-pounding moments where I *feel* that there is no way this gospel is not true and that this work is not true and God is not true and what we're working toward is not true. It's impossible.

I'm really grateful for those sometimes *rare* feelings to help me stay focused on why we're here and what we need to be doing. I'm grateful I have taken the time to write them down, so in the future when I don't feel that when I need it most, when I allow doubts to creep in longer than I should,

I am reminded of those *undeniable* times that I in reality felt *Him* through His spirit to bring me back.

Elder Ballard said, "I encourage you to stop and think carefully before giving up whatever it was that brought you to your testimony of the restored Church of Jesus Christ in the first place. Stop and think about what you have felt here and why you felt it. Think about the times when the Holy Ghost has borne witness to you of eternal truth" (M. Russell Ballard, "To Whom Shall We Go?" *Ensign*, Nov. 2016).

Can you think of a time where you felt the Spirit? Can you think of a time where you felt hope? Peace? Love, forgiveness, happiness, laughter, comfort? Because *all* things that are good *are* God showing Himself to us. All good things are from and because of Christ. I hope that every day we take time to notice Him because He is always there and we feel Him every day more than we recognize.

So yeah, maybe we do that all too familiar dance with the adversary, *but* then we have these moments in our life where we feel and experience *so deeply* that we have no words to describe exactly what happened or how we felt . . . but we just know that *electrifying* feeling is from God and from this gospel. A feeling that trumps *all* feelings of doubt or discouragement. No doubt can hold up against those feelings.

Refuse to let some pathetic attempt from the adversary take away from the reality of those times we have felt the Spirit. Where we have felt *Him*. Where we have felt our soul dancing within us. And I can't deny that every time I have felt those electrifying feelings, I was living the gospel. And I was seeking after Him.

Because I sure as heck never felt those goosebump moments that set my soul dancing *before* I got baptized.

Yeah, maybe things are hard, and maybe things aren't going how we had in mind, but just like today as I was pondering where I was when I first wrote this book, we will without a doubt look back and be grateful for where we are, what we went through to get there and what we've gained along the way, and we wouldn't want to change a thing. Let's do what we can to stay focused and try to create more moments where we invite the Spirit in our life that can allow us and our souls to *thrive* because *oh,* what a feeling! Let's vow to not forget or doubt them when they do come. Let's vow to not allow the adversary run rogue with our life and remember that we have the literal power to cast him out, a power he *has* to obey.

I hope you feel empowered with exactly who you are, exactly *where* you are. Because with God, you have *all* the power. Absolutely never forget who you are and *Whose* you are: a God who has all the power in existence on your side to help you succeed and become better and to conquer the world!

And you know what? The blessings in our life, even the hard and unexpected ones, are real blessings, from a real God, who really does love us, who really did handpick those exact things to help us succeed gloriously, and who is preparing a place in heaven for you *this exact moment.* No part of that is ordinary or insignificant. I'm not sure how it could make us feel anything but empowered.

YOUR SOUL IS ROOTING FOR YOU! And so is God. And so am I.

Let's embrace the unexpected knowing who is guiding us. Let's not allow anything or anyone alter the fact that we are God's and we are made for something so much greater than just what's here. We are His and *that is everything.* And if that isn't empowering, then I don't know what is.

So, as it turns out, in every situation, we have *everything* to celebrate.

And before I sign off, for what I imagine my last time for this book, I just wanted you to know that I'm really grateful for you. It's incredibly important to me, and I take great responsibility and pride in it, to be open and stay genuine and transparent all the time. My purpose to be online and to write and speak is very specific. None of this is about me or my book. It's about connecting with each other and laughing a lot and following God. It's about letting others know they aren't alone in their feelings of fatigue and wonder and doubt and anger and trials. And it's about helping each other home.

The way I see it, if we have shame in the feelings *we all have*—when we are embarrassed and silent in these feelings we all have—everyone loses. Since baptism, I have consistently written about the times I have felt ugly, when I felt I wasn't good enough, when I've felt abandoned by God, unemployed times, family turmoil, times of anguish, times of death and loss, times of severe loneliness, persecution, bad habits and struggles, as well as sacred experiences. I have been very specific of almost all of my challenges on my website. This book is in great detail of just my trials and how hard life is. My firesides are in great detail of those times I've wondered if He truly cares about us and those times when we feel our prayers are unanswered. But you're still here. I have laughed and hugged and talked and shed tears with so many of you. I have embraced and grown and strengthened from your experiences and emails and spirit you've shared with me.

And I just wanted to thank you. Thank you for reading. Thank you for listening. Thank you for connecting. For your emails. For your hugs. For your stories and testimony and honesty. For teaching me. For opening up to me. For your love. Your example. For showing up. Thank you for supporting the mission of helping others and showing them the reality of God. I appreciate you *so* much. I am better because of you. And I am sending love and prayers your way!

Isn't God just *oh so* good?

About the Author
AL CARRAWAY

AL CARRAWAY is a multi-award-winning LDS speaker, a convert, and author to *Cheers to Eternity*.

Al was born and raised in Rochester, New York, where she earned her degree in graphic design and marketing. She became a member of The Church of Jesus Christ of Latter-day Saints in 2009 and has since written about her relationship with God, her experiences, lessons, and trials on www.alcarraway.com. Since 2010, she has found herself traveling across the country every week speaking to LDS audiences of all kinds—those at youth camps, firesides, Time Out for Women, and even in prisons. Al shares her conversion story and teaches all those who will listen how to keep going in hard times and of the reality of God and this Church. Her passion is to tell everyone that happiness exists and that it comes from this gospel. She is a lover of the outdoors and waking up early. She is a taco enthusiast and is happiest when she is with her husband, Ben, and their two kids, Gracie and Christian.

Scan to Visit

alcarraway.com